# SKETCHES OF THE EYE

*Rachel A. Hall, Editor*

# Sketches of the Eye

Library of Congress
Cataloging in Publication Data

ISBN 0-7951-5095-4

Printed in China

Published by
The International Library of Photography
3600 Crondall Lane
Suite 101
Owings Mills, MD 21117

# FOREWORD

Writing about photography is a difficult task, as it entails the translation of one art form into another. While every photograph may not inspire a thousand words, it is easy to see how the saying evolved. Words are a function of the intellect. But, much like music, a visual image speaks directly to the emotions, evoking an immediate and powerful response. Only when one attempts to analyze, interpret, and critique this image do words come into play.

As one views a photograph, one is slowly taken on a visual journey through the eye of the photographer. Whether the photograph was staged or the "point-and-click method" was employed, the picture represents the fact that moments in time pass within the blink of an eye. The photographer not only captures a scene or a subject; he also creates a lasting, tangible image of a fleeting instant. The beauty of photography is that any individual can produce an image of these passing moments.

Photography represents both an active and a passive art form. The degree to which a photographer participates in his art form varies from photograph to photograph. The photographer can either tell a story within the photograph, or simply stand aside and record life as it happens. The one thing that holds true for all photography is this: without the photographer there can be no photograph. Even in a simple snapshot, the photographer's influence is clearly evident.

The photographs within this anthology exhibit their own importance as well as demonstrate the importance of the photographer. In some cases, the idea or photo found the photographer. For instance, while taking pictures on a nature hike, a photographer may catch the sunset as it breaks through a bunch of trees, and thus an idea may be born. In other instances, a photographer may orchestrate and choreograph the set-up of a photograph in order to fulfill a creative idea or notion. (This may be the case in still-life or abstract photography.)

Another similar element in most of these photographs is the photographer's love of and dedication to his subject. For example, nature photography is often captured by devoted nature watchers. Those people who take humorous photographs usually enjoy the lighter side of life and tend to look for the funniest aspect of any situation. The numerous photographs of children in this book were most likely taken by parents or grandparents who appreciate the joy and wonderment contained in a child's smile. Becoming emotionally involved with a subject, through deep love or interest, often enables a photographer to generate ideas that help him capture the true essence of his subject.

There are also photographers who gain inspiration not from relating to one specific subject or another, but rather from focusing on the photographic process itself. They often use special techniques to create images they have envisioned within their own minds, or they choose to concentrate on one particular aspect of photography (such as lighting) and through experimentation examine its effect on a particular subject. By casting aside conventional approaches, these photographers open different pathways to new ideas, allowing their own imaginations to roam freely.

No matter how or why a photograph is taken, the viewer must realize that each photograph represents an individual's artistic viewpoint. There are many excellent photographs contained in this anthology. At a quick glance they might appear to be just pictures, but be sure to focus on the ideas being conveyed, both emotionally and physically. Allow yourself to become lost in the photo: perhaps you may gain a new understanding of it, or you may simply be able to relate more deeply to the photographer's viewpoint.

Andy Warhol once predicted that in the future everyone will have his fifteen minutes in the spotlight. This philosophy could easily be applied to photography by simply stating that every subject has its moment, and as a photographer, one must strive to find and capture these instants. After all, these cherished moments, which may seem frozen in time when we see them through the camera's viewfinder, do not last fifteen minutes; rather, viewing a photograph that captures these instances may trigger memories that will always remain embedded deep within our minds. Through photographs we are therefore offered a physical reminder as an accompaniment to a memory. We then hold in our hands the permanency of a cherished moment in time—an image of yesterday.

**Russell Hall**
**Senior Editor**

# EDITOR'S NOTE

Of the five senses, the gift of sight is presumably the most valuable. It allows us to see thousands of different images a day and gives us an insight as to what the world is all about. Each and every sight taken in—prior to being photographed—can be considered a sketch by the human eye. Like sketches done on paper, these visual sketches are often hasty and undetailed. With photography, it is common to do quick sketches in your head of prospective scenes, sort of like a rough draft. In the end, however, there is always the option to enhance an image by taking into account lighting; the use of a telephoto lens; contrast, when working with black-and-white film; and the angle at which the picture is taken.

With the use of lighting and a telephoto lens, Raden Mohamed Hussein Jayman has managed to capture and enhance an exceedingly detailed image with his Grand Prize winning photograph, "Pumpkin Shoot." Several factors combined lend to the seemingly flawless composition of this photo-graph, but the light illuminating the background plays a key role. For one, it accentuates the simple black and green, producing a striking contrast. Second, it outlines the contour of the plant, making its curvy shape more apparent and setting it apart from the background. And third, it makes it possible to see an abundant amount of detail on the plant; and it is the detail that gives it dimension. This includes the web patterns on the leaves, the tiny fur-like hairs that trail along the perimeter of the leaves and stems, and the coiling plant shoots. The texture has been captured so well that as the viewer you just want to run your finger along the soft hairs or gently pull on the coil just to see it spring back. Jayman has done more than just capture a close-up portion of a pumpkin plant; with a little extra, yet simple, effort, he has magnificently transformed a common garden plant into a mystical entity.

Depending on the scene, some visualizations required more adjustments than others to heighten their overall effect. In Jayman's photo, the image would have turned out nearly invisible had he not used light. On the other hand, with a view as

spectacular as this, Martin Abelson didn't have to do much to enhance this scene, "On the Serengeti," his First Prize winning photograph. Here, the environment is naturally enhanced. The Serengeti Plain remains to be one of the last remaining wildlife spectacles on Earth, and in one shot, Abelson has captured its beauty, uncultivated manifestation, and untamed inhabitants. The plain itself appears to go on forever, hence the true meaning of Serengeti: endless plains.

At a first glance, "On the Serengeti" appears to be quite plain with its simple blue clouded sky and green grass, yet after a closer look it becomes altogether exquisite. From the foreground to the background, the color tones are doing just the opposite. The sky starts out with a very light shade of blue and proceeds to get darker as it blends in with the terrain, and the ground appears to be a darker green in front of the giraffes, only to turn into lighter shades of yellow the further back it goes. And because the entire scene was captured in focus, the blades of grass; the spots on the giraffes and their faces; the trees in the background; and the mountaintops peeking through the clouds are clearly visible. The two giraffes with their heads slightly touching add the finishing touch, giving it that picture-perfect quality.

One photograph that closely resembles that of an actual sketch is John Michael Lockwood's First Prize winning "Romy." Taken with black-and-white film, this image exposes only that which is necessary and simply wouldn't have the same dramatic effect if in color. Here, Lockwood has manipulated the black and white tones to enhance the image of Romy. Due to the extreme amount of

contrast in her face, the features of this girl appear overexposed, increasing the eccentricity of the photo, and a couple features are not even visible, namely her nose and chin. This technique is called using the whitest white and the blackest black. The one feature, however, that immediately draws attention are her eyes. Lined in black, slanted upwards, and completely captivating, they give her the look of a tigress. Along with her eyes, the eyebrows, lips, and the strand of hair alongside her face keep the extreme white balanced. Her face seems to be Lockwood's main focus, as her neck and shoulders have been left slightly out of focus. The leopard-print top enhances the unusual perspective of the photograph and adds a touch of charisma to it, while also adding some gray tones to lessen the contrast around her face.

The gift of sight is invaluable, and we should use it to its fullest to see and create sketches upon sketches in our minds. However, a sketch is just a sketch until some imagination is used to create a more appealing effect. In other words, a photographer has the option of taking a simple snapshot or doing a little something extra to embellish the shot, making it more visually appealing. With photography, one can never experiment enough.

I would like to congratulate all the winners of this contest and thank all the photographers for submitting their work. I wish all of you the very best in all of your future photographic endeavors. My appreciation and thanks go out as well to the entire staff here at the International Library of Photography for making the completion of this book possible. I would personally like to thank the editorial department, administrative staff, data entry and computer services personnel, customer service representatives, and mailroom staff for all their hard work and dedication.

**Rachel A. Hall**
**Editor**

# Grand Prize Winner

**Raden Mohamed Hussein Jayman**
*Pumpkin Shoot*

Nature

**April Greene**        Children
*I Do Myself*

**Shannon Stocker**        Humor
*Why Lawyers Are So Expensive*

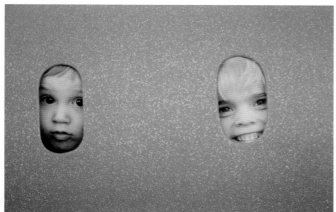

**Sherri Jones**        Children
*Here's Looking At You!*

**Xinyi Wu**        Portraiture
*My Dream*

**Caitlin Stevens**        Travel
*Mona Lisa*

**Lisa Jackson**        Children
*Daddy's Cap*

**Peter Jeffer**                    Portraiture
*Essence Of Emily*

**Matthew Field**                    Nature
*Zebra Love*

**Marsha Davis**                    Nature
*The Beauty Of A Winter Frost*

**Carl Rauschenberg**                    Action
*God's Hand At Work!*

**Vincent Falkowski**                    Nature
*Simply White*

**Ralph E. Norton**                    Other
*Untitled*

**Kevin St. Amour**      Children
*Quinn*

**Eric S. Feil**      Other
*Final Rest*

**Rick G. Miller**      Travel
*Wooden Horses, Tower Of London*

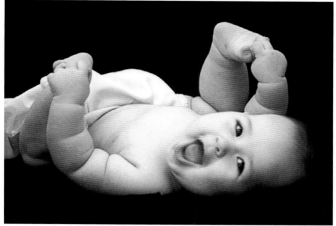

**Lisa Suzanne Harper**      Children
*Toes*

**Willard Overton**      Nature
*Morning Stretch*

**Manish Tokas Chaudhary**      Sports
*Pride Of India*

**Anthony Autumn Wolf Baldwin**  Other
*Empty Sky*

**Raymond Lei**  Travel
*Fifth Avenue Store Window*

**Raden Mohamed Hussein Jayman**  Nature
*Pumpkin Shoot*

**Savita Patil**  Children
*Innocence*

**Ken Howard Sullivan**  Animals/Pets
*Peeping Tom*

**Rozilynn C. Mitchell**  Other
*Do You Believe In Magic?*

**Jana Jean Jackson**                    Portraiture
*New Gloves*

**Wagner Santos**                    Children
*Brothers*

**Richard Lewis Judd**                    Children
*Untitled*

**Jamie Aaron Niekowal**                    People
*Cast No Shadow*

**Yolanda A. Daglio**                    Travel
*Little Sisters In The Andes*

**Patrick Boyer**                    Other
*Old Electric Trains In The South Of France*

**Wei Zhang**                          Portraiture
*Proud*

**Luzviminda Caasi Jayme**                    Sports
*Go-Carting To Remember*

**Jacek Polczynski**                        Nature
*Cholla*

**Mohammed Hyssain Al-Mashi**                Children
*Untitled*

**Robert Alan Fischer**                    Travel
*Trophies And Used Books*

**Chua Pei Shan**                      Animals/Pets
*A Dog's World*

**Thomas K. Schlup**  Sports
*Concentrate . . .*

**Neil Mackenzie**  Sports
*Hurricanes Rugby*

**Vickie Szumigala**  Other
*Thirty Rocks*

**Alan R. Keller**  Nature
*Huka Falls*

**Ashish Vansal**  Animals/Pets
*Untitled*

**Cem Topdemir**  People
*A Gathering*

**Corneliu Laurentiu Cazacu**      Nature
*The Wind Comb*

**Robert William Niesen**      Action
*Ridin' The Rocket At Disneyland*

**Jed Goode**      Animals/Pets
*Cat On A Pantile Roof*

**Enrico J. Miguelino**      People
*Punk Rock Professor*

**Brenda Tamar Berson**      Portraiture
*Untitled No. 3*

**Angel Alvarado**      People
*Rosario*

**Johann Frank**                                    Nature
*Butterfly*

**Raul Gaztelu**                                    Other
*Boats*

**Ariel Zusya Benjamin**                            Action
*War-Torn Sky Over Jerusalem*

**Danni Zhu**                                       People
*Cat*

**Hector Eli Gonzales**                             Nature
*Flower In Thailand*

**Ed P. Motley**                                    Humor
*Kayla Surprised*

**Laura Elizabeth Kearns**          People
*Untitled*

**Vesa E. Valtonen**          People
*Angel In Despair*

**Kyle James Baker-Scott**          Portraiture
*Untitled*

**David Alexander**          People
*Liquid Light*

**Zsolt Homonnai**          Portraiture
*Restrained Smile*

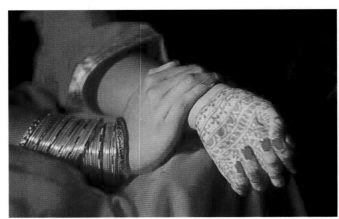

**Amin Rahim Khan**          Travel
*Beautiful Hands*

**Steve Lamb**
*Angel Eyes*
Other

**Antonio Presa Vazquez**
*Lone*
Travel

**Thomas M. Niccum**
*China Smoke*
Travel

**Alan Thomas Perella**
*Little One*
Children

**Tony Shuler**
*Carpenter Bee*
Animals/Pets

**Martin N. Abelson**
*On The Serengeti*
Travel

**David Robert Weisenbarger**          Portraiture
*Innocence*

**Michael Sandberg**          People
*Young Musician*

**Henry K. Fine**          People
*Coming Of Age In Papua New Guinea*

**Felipe G. Pereira**          Sports
*Going For The Goal*

**Aman Mehinli**          Action
*The Last Shot*

**Erica Renee Norman**          People
*Teen Angst*

**Laszlo A. Horvath**
*Untitled*
Humor

**John Michael Lockwood**
*Romy*
People

**Michael Sherman Notko**
*Maria*
Portraiture

**Jin Lin**
*This Is My Pet*
Animals/Pets

**Angel Lynn Wozniak**
*Untitled*
Other

**Rafael Guzman**
*Bulldog*
Animals/Pets

**Claudio Garbellini** Animals/Pets
*Quattro Chiacchere*

**Bernt Järnepalm** People
*Natascha*

**Arno Daalder** People
*Factory Worker Taking A Break*

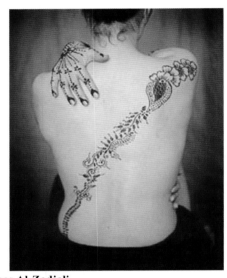

**Dina Abbas Al-Zadjali** People
*Henna*

**Eric Speelmon** Children
*Little Jedi Knight*

**Sommer Dawn Hatfield** Action
*Free*

**Crystal Sinclair Solsbak**　　　　　　　　Children
*So Much Love*

**Sorin Varzaru**　　　　　　　　Nature
*Critter Perspective*

**Alexandr Levin**　　　　　　　　Other
*Aliens*

**Rembert Giles Meszler**　　　　　　　　Humor
*Get Off My Head*

**Ute Kirchhoff**　　　　　　　　Portraiture
*My Lovely Sophie*

**Amanda R. Lents**　　　　　　　　Humor
*Tobacco*

**Maxim Sleptsov**                                    Humor
*Hello*

**Patanjali V. Parimi**                               Children
*Sravya*

**Ron Wierman**                                       Portraiture
*Prayer In G-Major*

**Rynol Inon Sarmon**                                 Action
*Fire Dance*

**Rene Guerrero**                                     Action
*The Standoff*

**Vinay Tiwari**                                      Sports
*Untitled*

**Sonny Poole** Animals/Pets
*No Fear*

**Estelle Jessica Park** Other
*Untitled*

**Boho Jin** Animals/Pets
*Untitled*

**Kim Young Jun** Portraiture
*Untitled*

**Roger Wayne Parker** Sports
*I'm Trying, Coach!*

**Donald M. Maffitt** Animals/Pets
*Mindy*

**Suzanne Carpenter**                    Animals/Pets
*Sleepy*

**Patrick J. Boening**                    Children
*So Funny . . .*

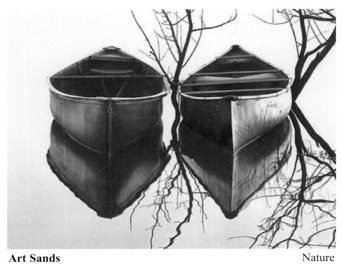

**Art Sands**                    Nature
*Two Guys Overboard*

**Edward Kenneth Flanagan**                    Other
*Dodge*

**Mark Webster Hurd**                    Travel
*Fossil Rim*

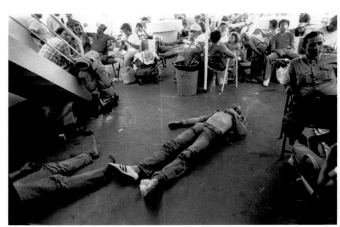

**Stelios Tsagris**                    Travel
*Sleeping On The Deck*

**Michael F. Oryl**     Travel
*Ferris Wheel At The Oktoberfest*

**Melissa Lee Hann**     Other
*The Other Side*

**Erik P. Olsen**     Sports
*Seaquam Football*

**Anatoliy I. Kazantsev**     Humor
*Keep Smiling*

**Andrew Sokov**     Portraiture
*Alsu*

**Nick Belhomme**     Portraiture
*Facial Fog*

**John R. Benson** Children
*Happiness*

**Robert Jurgens** People
*Firstborn*

**James Ware** Portraiture
*Angelina*

**Jim V. Coffey** Nature
*Ultimate Wisdom*

**Eleanor Bumbera** Travel
*Bow Lake*

**Marjorie Moreno** Nature
*A Petunia Bath*

**Norma Balaam**
People
*Personality Captured*

**Sanish Mondkar**
Travel
*Whale In San Diego Sea World*

**Kenneth Earl Nelson**
Travel
*Kuala Lumpur, Malaysia*

**Chris Matherne**
Nature
*Search For God*

**Tammy Demanche**
Children
*You Rake 'Em, I'll Play In 'Em!*

**Michael Earl Short**
People
*The Days Of Piracy*

**Chris J. Wehner**                                                 Nature
*Snake River And Canyon At Twin Falls, ID*

**Donna Staton**                                                 Children
*Austin Drew—Happy Baby*

**Tracy Lynn Hatton**                                        Portraiture
*I'll Be Your Huckleberry*

**Jackie Corder**                                                 Children
*Wyatt's First Caterpillar*

**Chandransu Choudhury**                                          Nature
*Untitled*

**Dawn Dicicco**                                            Animals/Pets
*Are You A Snow Dog?*

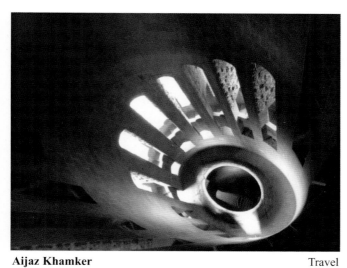

**Aijaz Khamker**          Travel
*Inside The Sagrada Familia—Barcelona, Spain*

**Beth Gilman**          Children
*Look Up, Sissy!*

**Kathryn Caro**          Travel
*Vapor Trails Ocotillo*

**Enrique Mora**          Travel
*The Trans-American Landmark Of Beautiful San Francisco*

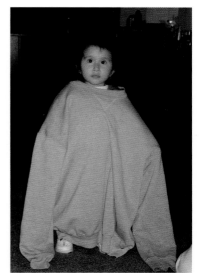

**Juan Lopez**          Children
*Beba In My Shirt*

**Pat Boone**          Animals/Pets
*Day Is Done*

**Darlene Ruiz**       Travel
*The Real Havana*

**Barb Muth**       Children
*Cheyenne*

**Tracey DeMello**       Nature
*American Bison*

**Elizabeth Smith**       Travel
*Ummmm, It's A Little Cold In There*

**Jason Buckwalter**       Nature
*Windy Day In Islamorada, FL*

**W. McDonald Lee**       Nature
*Nova Scotian Sky*

**Lynn Caldeiro**　　　　　　　　　　　　　　　Nature
*Autumn Geese*

**Michael Bernhard**　　　　　　　　　　　　　Travel
*Untitled*

**Grace Hunt**　　　　　　　　　　　　　　　Children
*Young Travelers, Sierra And Joshua*

**Tresa Spring**　　　　　　　　　　　　　　People
*My Girls*

**Roger Carlson**　　　　　　　　　　　Animals/Pets
*Nice Body Pillow—Hopefully It Won't Wake Up!*

**Ting Qian**　　　　　　　　　　　　　　　Children
*Smile On A Snowy Day*

**Sharon Steinmetz** Children
*Are You Talkin' To Me?*

**Seth Leonard** Nature
*Three Surfers*

**Lucie Ayala** Nature
*Wedding Flowers*

**Stanley Stern** Nature
*Tucson Winter Sundown*

**Angela Phillips** Children
*Jordan Crashed*

**Lindy Swarthout** Nature
*Distant Bridge—Yosemite Valley*

**Mary Niederlander** Children
*Sometimes We All Need A Little Steering In The Right Direction*

**Karen Burton** Animals/Pets
*Friendship*

**David Hatcher** Children
*One, Two, Three, Lift*

**Meghann Eppstein** Children
*Red Bar*

**Annette Lake** Travel
*Winter Fun*

**June Jewell** Children
*Cuties*

**Dave White**        Nature
*Snow On The Way*

**Lori Leytham**        People
*Homecoming Court 2000*

**Nancy Stebbins**        Children
*I'm Such A Ham!*

**Margaret Tranggono**        Animals/Pets
*Untitled*

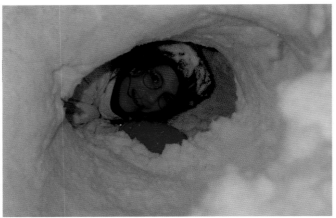

**David Virzi**        Children
*Exploring A New Home!*

**Chris Budka**        Action
*First Swim*

**Robin Barnes** Children
*Dadda, I Broke It*

**Stacey Pieters** Animals/Pets
*Mmm, Tuna Sandwich, My Favorite!*

**Annelise Capon** Travel
*Bowen Falls Splash With Joy After Their Long Descent From Mitre Peak, NZ*

**Amy Parker** Children
*A Break From Winter*

**Jeffrey Jones** Travel
*Noah's Snow*

**Candace Coram** Travel
*Sunrise At PTI*

**Shankar Iyer**                                    Animals/Pets
*The Lonely Ugly Duckling*

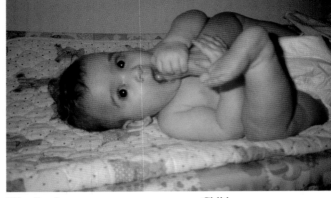

**Kim Snyder**                                    Children
*Tasty Little Toes*

**Laura Rudek**                                    People
*New Dad*

**Diane Vellner**                                    Children
*Nap For Two*

**Dayle Prue**                                    Travel
*Untitled*

**Emily Countryman**                                    Animals/Pets
*Pink Puppy*

**Jennifer Chaplin**                    Nature
*Arizona Cactus*

**James Russ**                    Children
*Easter Sunday Celebration*

**Jennifer Burke**                    Children
*Kyle And Kaylee*

**Chad Short**                    Animals/Pets
*Lazy Cat*

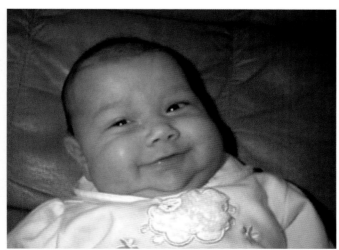

**Brenda Boykin**                    Humor
*Shana*

**Robbie Fisher**                    Travel
*Sunflowers Near Cognac, France*

**Jon Hersey**                                    Travel
*A Relaxing Walk On Liberty In Otaru, Japan*

**Jennifer Wraspir**                              Other
*Veteran's Day Vision*

**Kathleen Pryor**                                Travel
*Postcard Sky Over Palermo*

**Connie McCool**                                 Children
*Cookie Monsters!*

**Julianne Prekaski**                             Children
*Lily With Flowers*

**Jesse Lolley**                                  People
*My New Bride*

**Maria Myers**                              Children
*They Won't Find Me Under Here*

**Bonnie Janks**                             Children
*Caitlyn Helps Fix My Nose*

**Michelle Barnard**                         Children
*First Snowfall*

**Julie Duarte**                             Children
*My Big Brother*

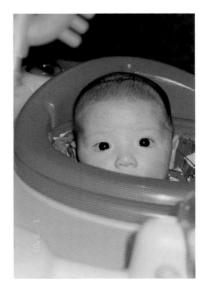

**Grace Becker**                             Children
*A Deer In Headlights*

**Rosemary Moon**                            Children
*I Did It!*

**Carol W. Barnes**                    Children
*Ballet And Boots—Nowhere But Texas!*

**Prabal Bhattacharya**                    Portraiture
*Contemplate*

**Maureen C. Davis**                    Children
*Cousins Having A Ball*

**Terri Lynam**                    People
*Fixing The Vacuum Cleaner*

**Radith Turnure**                    Travel
*Argus-Matchmatic*

**Robin Sheheane**                    Children
*Halloween Scarecrows*

**Julie Kennedy**                              Animals/Pets
*Annie Always Finds The Best Spot*

**Veronica Walters**                              Other
*The Omnipotent Osier*

**Robin Davis**                              Children
*We Are Mom's Silly Bunnies*

**Greg Ocdinaria**                              Travel
*Naturally Beautiful*

**Marilou Geverola**                              Travel
*Flames On Mirage*

**Eileen Bader**                              Animals/Pets
*Elijah Blue's Bath!*

**Thomas Moyer**                                              Action
*It's All Downhill From Here!*

**Sudheer Vijayakumar**                                      Travel
*Rings*

**Venkatesh Sadagopan**                                     Nature
*The White Woods*

**Francis Firmalo II**                                       Nature
*Solitude*

**Carol Kelly**                                            Children
*Playing In The Window*

**Charles Wisniewski**                                       Travel
*Montauk Lighthouse—Fall 2000*

**Matt Greiner and Cheri Bass**   Animals/Pets
*We Are So Sleepy*

**Lisa Weissman**   Children
*Waist High To A Munchkin On The Morning After The Storm*

**Frank Mattos**   Animals/Pets
*Fish Fascination*

**Kyle Masiello**   Travel
*Paris Hotel In Las Vegas*

**Nicole Beard**   Children
*I Love Sports!*

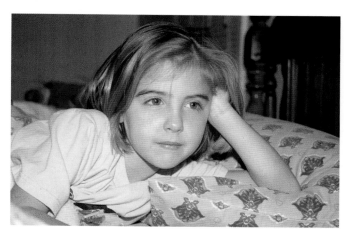

**Diana Dail**   People
*A Whole Day Ahead With Mommaw—What Shall We Do?!*

**Denise Heggan**        Children
*I Love You!*

**Rhonda McClintock**        Nature
*Sunset At Sea*

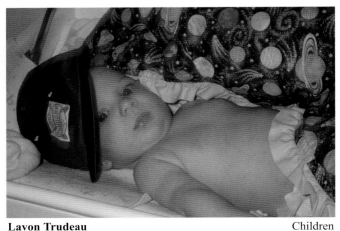

**Lavon Trudeau**        Children
*Lake Trudeau*

**Norman Smith**        Nature
*Oklahoma Ice Storm*

**Larry Miller**        Travel
*Ipanema Beach—Rio De Janeiro At Sunrise*

**Meloni Gursky**        Travel
*Being Silly*

**Dennis Marion** Travel
*Soho In NYC*

**Rosie Velasquez** Children
*Sisterhood*

**Wendy Reynolds** Children
*Baby Escargot*

**Jamin Roth** Animals/Pets
*Fritz In The Corn Crib*

**Karen Whiteway** Animals/Pets
*Punkin Relaxing In The Sun*

**Natalie Marioni** Travel
*Rooftops Of St.-Cirq-Lapopie, France*

**Gregg Shapiro**                                        Nature
*Simple Paradise*

**Heather Mitchell**                                     Children
*Sitting Up Is Great Fun!*

**Lori Pease-Stevens**                                   Children
*Doctor:  Does It Hurt When I Do This?*

**Eric Hill**                                            Animals/Pets
*Rosa Belle Tells Katie Martin To Hush!*

**Vanessa Salvia**                                       Children
*Candy Frenzy!*

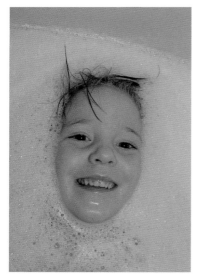

**Stephanie Bloomfield**                                 Children
*Bubble Girl*

**Benoit Chaffanjon**                                   Children
*Ben And Max On The Ski Slopes*

**Tara Barich**                                   People
*Steve And The Rock*

**Randy Knuckles**                                   Travel
*Warming Hut*

**Sheila Jones**                                   People
*First Party!*

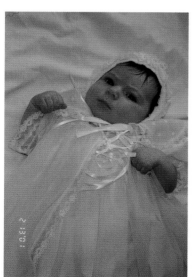

**Juliana Panetta**                                   Children
*Our Angel Is Baptized*

**Christine Curtin**                                   Animals/Pets
*Sadie On The Trail*

**Deb Krueger**                    Children
*Cute Friends!*

**Kathryn Henry**                    Children
*Waiting For Santa*

**Jacqueline Biles**                    Animals/Pets
*Best Friends Just Hanging*

**Heather Roderick**                    Travel
*My First Train*

**Hugo Perez**                    People
*Brenda Times Five Años*

**Suzanne Thompson**                    Children
*Junior Photographer*

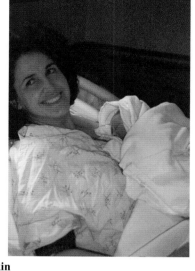

**Barbara Kernan** Sports
*Yes! My First Seven-Point Buck Deer*

**JoAnn Rankin** People
*Joy Of Birth*

**Angie Mosley** Other
*Tulip Tree In Spring*

**Elizabeth Hostetler** Sports
*Future Baseball Player!*

**Bill Farrell** Children
*Sticky Grandson*

**Teri Halasz** Children
*Baby Fat*

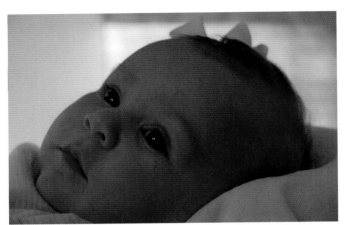

**Sheila Richburg**  Portraiture
*Ashlon*

**Michael Ivan Schwartz**  Travel
*Atlantic City Sunset*

**Rhonda Lindner**  Animals/Pets
*He Loves Me, He Loves Me Not . . .*

**Missy Gegenheimer**  Animals/Pets
*Wanna Play?*

**Todd Franken**  Sports
*Skydive To Live!*

**Tami Beccaria**  Children
*Summer Smiles*

**Michele Moscovitz**　　　　　　Animals/Pets
*Sophie Dressed As Barney*

**Becky Dray**　　　　　　Children
*I Love Dressing Up!*

**Tracy Wanty**　　　　　　Children
*Sunday Drive*

**Sandra Wolf**　　　　　　Animals/Pets
*Catching Some Rays—Indoor Sunbathing*

**Bronwyn Madison**　　　　　　Animals/Pets
*O Give Me A Home*

**Cindy Krenke**　　　　　　Nature
*Like Stalactites In A Cave, The Icicles Cling To Our House!*

**Sandeep Kishore**                                                          People
*Fully Loaded*

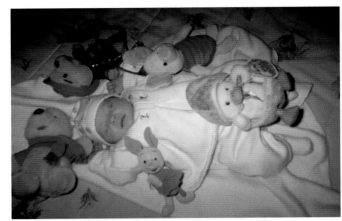

**Ephraim Garcia**                                                          Travel
*Grandpa's Pride, Kaylina, Pure Daughter Of Light*

**Jeanne Everhart**                                                          Travel
*Rolling Hills*

**Joi Gayre**                                                          Children
*Christmas Basket*

**James Tharpe**                                                          Animals/Pets
*Do Not Look Down . . . Please Do Not Look Down*

**Kathleen Jensen**                                                          Children
*Grapes, Please!*

**Sheryl Isenhart**                                          Children
*Sarah And Her Horse*

**Susan Feibel**                                          Travel
*Bay Palms Golf Course—MacDill AFB, FL*

**Taeho Im**                                          Sports
*End Of A Perfect Day!*

**M. Nancy Pasnik**                                          Nature
*Double Rainbow*

**Benoit Chaffanjon**                                          Children
*Amazing Christmas Tree*

**Maria Sanders**                                          Children
*I Am The Champion*

**Brian Ardel**                                   Nature
*Seascape, Andres Island*

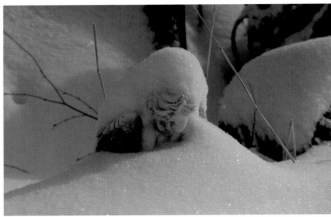

**Sasha Fernandes**                               Nature
*Angel's Blanket*

**Joseph Dangerfield**                     Animals/Pets
*Startled Yorkies*

**Ron Shultz**                                  Children
*Cassie And Abbey*

**Michelle dos Santos**                    Animals/Pets
*A Horse Of Course!*

**Regina Pregge**                                 Nature
*When The Sun Went Down In Georgia!*

**Dewi Wandansari** Nature
*Waves*

**Kevin Weaver** Travel
*Mendocino Through My Eyes*

**Greg McBride** Other
*Iron Age No. 16*

**Maggie Takita** Children
*Look At Me . . . A Regular Renoir*

**David Carlton** Children
*Best Friends*

**Glen Kerby** Children
*Mighty In Spirit*

**Linda McCoin**
*Downtown Los Angeles*
Travel

**Elizabeth Dawes**
*Windows Of Eze, France*
Travel

**Richard and Kim Kirchmeyer**
*The Dangers Of Skiing*
Travel

**Monica Zittle**
*A First Taste Of Snow*
Children

**Robin Phillips**
*Coleman River*
Nature

**Ralph Sherman**
*Oooh, Baby, It's Cold Outside*
Nature

**Barbara Kunkel**                                                              Travel
*Sunrise In The Desert*

**Suzanne Ward**                                                              Children
*Stay-At-Home Dad!*

**Roxanne Nosal**                                                              Nature
*A Day At Big Sur*

**Mikial Zultoski**                                                              Humor
*Look Out!*

**Chantal Sukel**                                                              Travel
*Menacing Skies, Ruins By The Sea—Tulum, Mexico*

**Jodi Hoskins**                                                              Other
*Woven Villa*

**Tara Cruser-Moss**                                    Animals/Pets
*Sure, I Wear Ralph Now And Then*

**Vicki Cupit**                                              Sports
*The Littlest Bulls Fan—Michael, Age Thirteen Months*

**Amy Weissenburger**                                   Animals/Pets
*Ears*

**Rachael Czepyha**                                        Children
*Helen's Smile*

**Penni Vachon**                                           Children
*Little Miss Hailie Jenna*

**Kristy Skaggs**                                            Nature
*Waterfall In Butterfly Sanctuary At Tama Zoo, Japan*

**Jim and Tina Skrocki**　　　　　　　　　Children
*What A Funny Face!*

**Billy Dale**　　　　　　　　　Nature
*Sky On Fire*

**Jennifer Sulton**　　　　　　　　　Children
*Just Having A Little Fun*

**Dana Weir**　　　　　　　　　Humor
*Untitled*

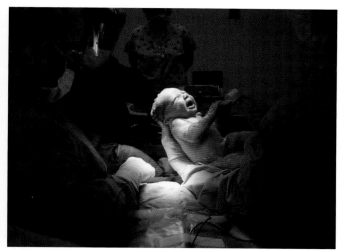

**Perry Cahill**　　　　　　　　　Children
*First Cry*

**Rubens Monteiro**　　　　　　　　　Portraiture
*The Old Well, A Symbol Of The University Of North Carolina At Chapel Hill*

**Michelle Alexander**                    Children
*My First Taste Of A Flower*

**Larry Chambers**                    Travel
*Mississippi River At Memphis*

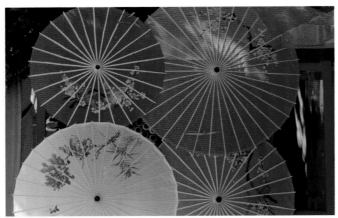

**James Johnson**                    Other
*Waiting For The Sun*

**Angelina Penso**                    Children
*First Taste Of Cake*

**Richard Bingham**                    Other
*My Two Angels*

**Brenda Karika**                    Nature
*Lake Ontario In Winter*

**Camille Richardson** Travel
*Hombre De Fantasia*

**Steven Murray** Children
*A Day At Camp*

**Kirsten Carter** Animals/Pets
*Not Now, I Am Relaxing*

**Kristy Lima** People
*Hey, Good-Lookin'!*

**Ted Thompson** Animals/Pets
*Miss Kitty*

**Shobhit Kapoor** People
*Untitled*

**Lina Willis**                                    Children
*Aiden Of The Jungle*

**Maria Galman**                              Animals/Pets
*I Am Innocent*

**Annette McRay**                                     Nature
*Summer Beauty*

**Sandie Lynch**                                    Children
*How Purrrrfect!*

**Tanja Lijffijt**                                       Travel
*Small Car, Big Bike!*

**Diana Nash**                                      Children
*Sara And Cassidy*

**Jessie Nalpathanchil**                                      Other
*Garden Of Good And Evil*

**Sara Ricalton**                                             Action
*Playing Hard*

**Charles Weatherholt**                                       Nature
*Sarasota Sun*

**Cheryl Coco**                                               Children
*Let It Snow*

**Donna Zahn**                                                Children
*Rock And Roll!*

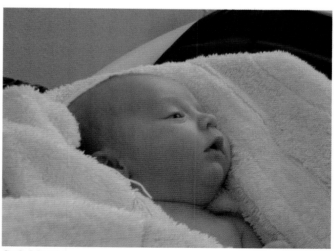

**Seth Martin**                                               Children
*After A Bath*

**Heidi Bajurin**                                         Animals/Pets
*Baby Giraffe On The Lookout*

**Aileen Qiu**                                              Children
*A Little Smiley*

**Maureen Gomes**                                          Sports
*Jaromir Jagr At Pre-Game Warm-up (Panthers Versus Penguins)*

**Walter Chung**                                            Travel
*Going Nowhere Fast*

**Grace Blake**                                            Nature
*Putting My Ducks In A Row*

**John Holmes**                                             Travel
*Atlantic Ocean—The Other Side*

**Joe and Barbara Short**     Travel
*Majestic Mt. Rainier, Washington*

**Bao Z. Hu**     Other
*Save Our Mother Earth—Sustainable Architecture*

**Rayanne Moore**     Children
*Dad's Girl*

**Peter Herbst**     Travel
*Kuranda Train—Australia*

**Mary Stambaugh**     People
*Grandma And Becca Lin*

**Karan Gryskiewicz**     Sports
*Karan's Bike*

**Joan Thompson**                    Children
*Dinner At A Restaurant*

**Michele Stephenson**          People
*Baby David*

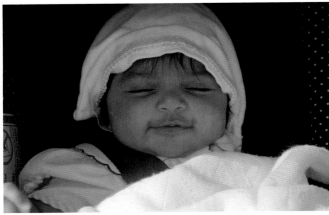

**Sagar Manne**                   Children
*I Am Dreaming!*

**John Small**                   Travel
*Interior Of The Dome Of St. Peter's In Rome, Italy*

**Sharon Midgett**            Children
*I've Got My Fishing Hat On, So Let's Go Fishing!*

**Geri Desousa**              Other
*Chloe And Casino*

**Lisa Schnell**                    Portraiture
*Look, No Pillows To Lean Against*

**Kristen Sharpe**                    Children
*A Patient Little Girl With A Squiggly Little Brother*

**Holly Halcumb**                    Children
*Poor, Poor Pitiful Me!*

**Aricka Martinez**                    Children
*Pre-Diva*

**Stephanie Lawson**                    Travel
*Golden Sunset*

**Nicole Eisen**                    Nature
*Drizzling Tree*

**Patti Meyer** Children
*Fussy Face*

**Dheeraj Agarwal** Nature
*Summer Love At Yosemite*

**Lina Palma** Travel
*Lake Tahoe*

**Rochelle Wightman** Humor
*Love Whipping Cream*

**John Magluyan** Travel
*Red Rock Sedona Sky*

**Keri Osterhout** Nature
*No Birds Were Hurt In The Making Of This Photo*

**Betty Harris** Humor
*Let It Snow, Let It Snow, Let It Snow!*

**Daryl Pepper** Children
*Oh, No! There Goes That Broom Again*

**Jill Hirsch** Animals/Pets
*Mommy And Ten-Day-Old Baby At Chicago Area Brookfield Zoo*

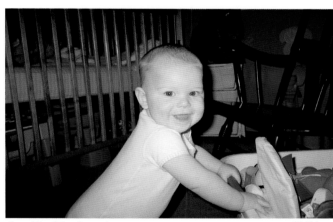

**Jennifer Woodward** Children
*So Cute*

**John Ramsey** Children
*Drummer*

**Therese Stick** Children
*My Free-Spirited Seventies Girl*

**Michelle Taylor** Children
*Mountain Sunflowers*

**Ginny Fischer** Travel
*Arlington National Cemetery*

**Marilou Abruscato** Nature
*My Husband And Cherry Blossoms—My Two Favorite Things!*

**Laura McGinnis** Children
*Naptime*

**BJ Santos** Children
*Christa & BJ*

**Tracie Fife** Children
*Cape Cod Coddette*

**Sharon Rickards**　　　　　　　　Children
*The Next Joe Montana*

**Traci Shields**　　　　　　　　Children
*After A Long Day, She Is So Sweet!*

**Teresa Plaza**　　　　　　　　Humor
*Beach Size Roll*

**Cindy Williams**　　　　　　　　Animals/Pets
*Yoshi*

**David Young**　　　　　　　　Travel
*Niagara Falls At Night*

**Christina Hall**　　　　　　　　Animals/Pets
*I Love You, Mommy!*

**Jeanie Lafferty**                                   Animals/Pets
*Lazy Beanbag Dog*

**Catherine Schultz**                                   Children
*Sydney Jo's First Time In Her Highchair*

**Jeff Jones**                                   Nature
*Malibu Spring*

**Staci Thomson**                                   Children
*Stop And Smell The Flowers!*

**Melanie Alexander**                                   Children
*Pouting Emily Rose*

**Marcie May**                                   Children
*Ovilee—Chole May Boo*

**Donald Miller**                                       Other
*Iron Horse*

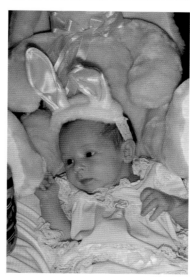

**Dina Bakalik**                                        Children
*Easter 2001*

**Camille Martin**                                      Children
*Little Girl In A Sea Of Blue*

**Maryann Corry**                                       Nature
*Cape Hatteras, NC, Awaiting Hurricane Irene—October 16, 1999*

**Cheryl Blaise**                                       Children
*Static Baby*

**Gail Cambareri**                                      Portraiture
*Teen Angel*

**Jeanette Oberholtzer**        Nature
*Magical Web*

**Anne Marie Phillips**        Children
*Sweetness*

**Marcel van Duren**        Other
*World Trade Center*

**Kenneth Earl Nelson**        Travel
*Chinese Temple*

**Gabrielle Dawn Goodman**        Nature
*Miller Beach Sunset*

**Joan C. Pawlowski**        Children
*You'd Better Be Good*

**Rhonda K. Elpers**                    Animals/Pets
*Rain Day*

**Saravana Sundar Kayarkanni Selvatharasu**          Portraiture
*God's View*

**Cathy Lynn Battle**                    Children
*No Greater Love Than Grand Love*

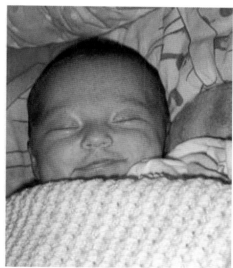

**Beverly Ann Weisbender**                    Children
*Sweet Dreams*

**Linda A. Bernardi**                    Portraiture
*Mother And Child At Sunset*

**Linda Irene Pearson**                    Nature
*River In Soo Valley—Cougar Mountain, Whistler, BC*

**Diana S. Meyer**          Animals/Pets
*Going Up*

**Leslie Anne DaSilva**          Animals/Pets
*Computer Cat*

**Angelique Martins**          Animals/Pets
*Itchie*

**Damon Neil Hudson**          Travel
*River Street—Savannah, GA*

**Courtney C. Flynn**          Nature
*Eastside Sunset*

**Rachel Brazil**          Children
*Baby And Her Kitty*

**Michele Renee Riley**                    Children
*Sleeping Beauty*

**Juanita Marie Mishler**                    People
*The Fog Is Lifting*

**Raúl Balsategui**                    Nature
*Dream*

**Brad Loni Ketsdever**                    Nature
*Lost And Alone*

**Michelle Brigette Fontenot**        Animals/Pets
*Lazy Dog*

**Jo Munro**                    Animals/Pets
*Ted E. Munro*

**Amy Michelle Hicks**  Animals/Pets
*Stormy*

**Robbie E. Bogan**  Children
*New Mom, New Baby*

**Rowan Drayton**  Portraiture
*Jo Munro At Ashcombe Maze—Melbourne, Australia*

**Matthew Emerson Kelly**  People
*Andy, Repose At Briggs Lake*

**Valerie Marie Martin**  Nature
*Driveway Out In Snowstorm*

**Haukur Thorolfsson**  Nature
*The Albatross Flies Into The Sunset*

**Shelly Rowe**        Children
*Aren't I Cute?*

**Monica J. Pechal**        Other
*The Old Gin*

**Dave Dieringer**        Nature
*The Lake*

**Tina Marie Gehrig**        Children
*Tyler The Raccoon*

**Keri Saville**        Animals/Pets
*What Are You Looking At?*

**Nicholas M. Ott**        Animals/Pets
*Kitten In A Basket*

**Edward Martin Pratt**
Nature
*Red Cloud Pass*

**Antonio Bruno Pandolfini**
Animals/Pets
*Peek-A-Boo*

**Cyndi Rena Schoen**
Children
*Heavenly*

**William Oldham**
Other
*Cannon At Old State House*

**Connie L. Bonds**
Nature
*Texas In Spring*

**David Kimberly Nagel**
Nature
*Sunday Morning Ride*

**Orlando Rodriguez**                                        People
*Reflections Of Beauty*

**Lisa Bilyj**                                              Travel
*Maui Sunset*

**Haley Caron Trott**                                      Children
*Baby's First Christmas*

**Kelly Louis Larson**                                      Nature
*Sunset Reflections*

**Jamie Diane Harris**                                      Nature
*Tree Truck*

**Laurie L. Sevin**                                        Children
*Sisters Are Forever*

**Peggy D. Jones**                                    Nature
*Pelicans*

**Gerald LeRoy Moore**                          Animals/Pets
*My Son Nicky*

**Mary Catherine McBride**                      Children
*A Walk On The Beach*

**Steve Gary Maushardt**                        Animals/Pets
*My Pot Of Gold*

**Matthew Soren Cox**                            People
*Window Girls*

**James William Stewart**                        People
*Sunrise*

**Jesper Hansen**  Animals/Pets
*Dendrobates*

**Tim J. Deering**  Nature
*Evening On The St. Lawrence*

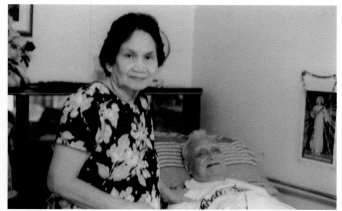

**Toni-Lynne Willkom Chai**  People
*Grandma & Grandpa*

**Diane Dellasala**  Travel
*Lookout Mountain Road—Golden, CO*

**Wendy L. Linscheid**  Animals/Pets
*The Boys*

**Gabriele Orsini**  People
*Hey*

**Patricia Jean Cullen**　　　　　　　　　Nature
*My Japanese Tree*

**Daren Harlow Spencer**　　　　　　　　Other
*Geiser Grand*

**Holly Nichole Brandon**　　　　　　Animals/Pets
*Moose In Action*

**Sherlynn A. Miller**　　　　　　　　　Nature
*Mighty Niagara*

**Andy DeMeo**　　　　　　　　　　　　Nature
*Sunset*

**Elias Santiago-Christian**　　　　　　　Travel
*Monument To The Puerto Rican Jibaro*

**Katalin Harris**        Nature
*Assateague Beach*

**Bridget Alleen Giovale**        Animals/Pets
*No More Pictures*

**Donald F. Wood**        Travel
*The Lady Welcomes*

**Mandy Rachelle Gray**        Children
*Hayley And Her Snow Bear*

**Angela Lynn Bartholomew**        Children
*We Have A Plan!*

**Dawn Michelle Bass**        People
*Man On Bike*

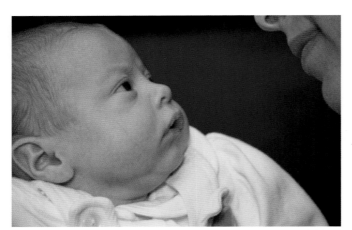

**Tom DeGerlia**                                   Children
*Mutual Admiration*

**Edd Voss**                                        Nature
*Utah Ranch In Winter*

**Mohan Kumar Mani**                               People
*Three Generations*

**RoxAnn Lyvonne Manley**                          Children
*Let Me Out*

**Carroll Marie Bastow**                           Animals/Pets
*Soaring Above*

**Tasha J. Larsen**                                People
*Contrast*

**Peter Charles Beck**                    Animals/Pets
*Dog In Mirror*

**Lauren Kimberly Juergens**              Travel
*Road To The Duomo*

**Jennifer Joy Rubright**                 Travel
*Home Is Where The Heart Lies*

**Wesley K. Harper**                      Travel
*Passing Through Newark At One Hundred MPH*

**Denny Edward Philipps**                 Nature
*Niagara*

**Tonie M. Mason**                        Children
*Spring Is Here*

**Kristy Welker**          Animals/Pets
*Rupert*

**Darrell Duane Arnold**          Nature
*Over The Falls*

**Richard Matthew Nemish**          Nature
*Squirrel Man*

**Linda M. Ruilova**          Nature
*After The Storm*

**Elizabeth Ann Deem**          Nature
*Teton Reflection*

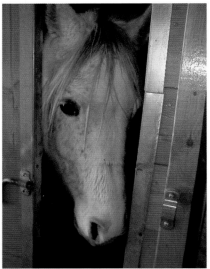

**Heather Nicole Pietrobono**          Animals/Pets
*Inquisitive Jade*

**Cindy Venettozzi**                    Animals/Pets
*Ya Know, I Used To Be A Contender*

**Henry Harms**                    Children
*Hmm . . . Heavy . . . Ughhh*

**Marvin R. Odor**                    Nature
*Divi-Divi By The Ocean*

**Clarence Raymond McGinnis**                    Nature
*Looking At Nature Through A Wagon Wheel*

**Cheryl Thrall**                    Other
*A Story To Tell*

**Chrystie Ann Kaipoleihulumanu Lee Ellswick**                    Children
*Lil' Mama In Training*

**Ginger R. Davies**                                          Children
*Who Is That Looking At Me?*

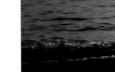

**Konstantin Vasilevich Kravtsov**                      Nature
*Evening*

**Nancy Jo Strankowski**                              Children
*Bath Time Campers*

**Jennifer Sheila Robinson**                          Children
*Sarah*

**Jose M. Perez**                                     Children
*Police Kid*

**Melodie Anne Watts**                                Children
*Friends At Christmas*

**Vichai Anudtarapanya**          Nature
*Lives*

**Rick Hursey**          Sports
*Rafting In The Colorado River*

**Chai Kongwei**          Action
*Street Activity*

**Joel Benjamin Bliss**          Other
*Serenity*

**Yazdie Noshir Panthaki**          People
*Faces Of Innocence From Vrindavan*

**Dana Renee Groshans**          People
*Sunshine Smile*

**David Erel**　　　　　　　　　　　　　Nature
*Autumn's Beauty*

**Karen Lea Jones-Hetland**　　　　　Animals/Pets
*Luka Lea, Angel Of Kittens*

**Susan J. Baricko**　　　　　　　　　　Travel
*Splendor In Barbados*

**Richard Shawn Manis**　　　　　　　Nature
*Sunset*

**Wendy L. Christophe**　　　　　　　Nature
*Easter Storm*

**Michele Lynn Deal**　　　　　　　Children
*Lesleyanne And Tobykitty*

**Joel B. Harleman**                                         Other
*Time*

**Eileen Waldrop**                                          Nature
*Sunset On The Lake*

**Gwendolen Rae Coulter**                               Children
*First Snow*

**Cindy A. Lange**                                          Nature
*Cold Duck*

**Shi Ann Dean**                                          Children
*Love*

**Lisa Marie Butcher**                                      Other
*Keeping An Eye On The Summer Surf*

**Corinne H. Chanmane**　　　　　　　　　　　Other
*Liberty Sunset*

**Mike Thomas Fuchs**　　　　　　　　　　　Sports
*Red Devils*

**Charlotte Elaine Souder**　　　　　　　　　Nature
*Hoover Dam*

**Alfonso Sudentas**　　　　　　　　　Animals/Pets
*Who, Me?*

**Sundee Jo Mahone**　　　　　　　　　　　Travel
*Sunset In Hawaii*

**Andy M. Santelli**　　　　　　　　　Animals/Pets
*Aussie Eyes*

**Jack Stephan**    Children
*So This Is Love*

**Shannon Marie Young**    Animals/Pets
*Hide-And-Seek*

**H. Penny McCoy**    Other
*The Egg*

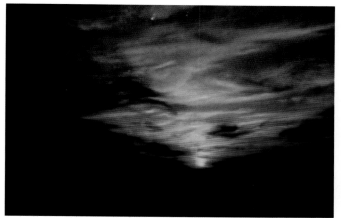

**Sheila J. Basil**    Nature
*Smokey Sunset*

**Michael Wayne Williams**    Other
*Ansel Adams*

**Loretta K. Cross**    Children
*Fall Eyes*

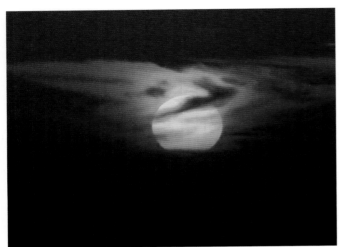

**Steven Roscoe Reed**                          Nature
*Shired Island Sunset*

**Mike Brown**                                  Nature
*Sunset Del Mar*

**Michael Allen King**                          Nature
*Clouds*

**Pat Vela**                                    Travel
*Oregon Sunset*

**Maria Manzanares**                            People
*Afloat*

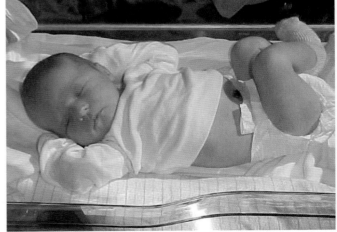

**Chaneque Rhapsody Connolly**                  Children
*Precious Baby Jake*

**Heather Marie Vandiver**                    Children
*Four Little Pumpkins*

**Brandy Lee McConaughey**                    People
*Beth At The Lake*

**Paul Roderick Williams**                    Nature
*Sundown In Norway*

**Carina Ann Fogelberg**                    Animals/Pets
*How To Catch A Bird*

**Maria Elena Franco**                    Children
*Treasures Are Everywhere*

**Jackie Michelle Graham**                    Nature
*Spring River*

**Kathy Shear**                                          Children
*Did You See That?*

**Arlie M. Wilkerson**                                   Nature
*Buffalo In The Tetons*

**Clifford Karpinski**                                   Nature
*Rangeley Lake Sunset*

**Megan Lynn Kern**                                      Other
*Musical Reflection*

**Stefenes So**                                          Children
*The Restful Evening*

**Sue Ann Kinney**                                       Children
*Who Says I Can't Fill My Daddy's Shoes!*

**Alice B. Guier**  People
*Sam Houston*

**Teresa Fernandez**  Animals/Pets
*Benji*

**Carol M. Germain**  Children
*Mutual Love*

**Nathar Ray McFarlain**  Travel
*Cajun Cabin*

**Diana Kay Gibson**  Nature
*Sunset On Lake Cumberland*

**Barbara Jean Hickey**  Animals/Pets
*Tami's Favorite Pose*

**Joel D. Kroon**                                          Nature
*Sunset In Florida*

**David Gene Williams**                                    Travel
*Downtown Glow*

**Joe T. Sparkman**                                        Nature
*Arkansas Ice 2000*

**Vladimir Houfek**                                        Action
*Air France*

**Robert Albert Hornyak**                                  Nature
*Walking A Tightrope*

**Rogelio Alberto Anguizola**                              Nature
*God's Finger*

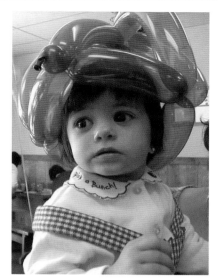

**Suzanne Linn Bernardi**　　　　　　Children
*First Birthday*

**Robert Kramer Jr.**　　　　　　Nature
*Texas Sunrise*

**Barbara Quigley**　　　　　　Children
*Family Camping Trip*

**Heidi Marie Main**　　　　　　Nature
*Redrock, Colorado*

**Daniel Paul Meltzer**　　　　　　Children
*Caution—Kids At Work*

**Scott Richard Southurst**　　　　　　Other
*F/A-18 Sunset*

**Ron C. Medcalf**  Nature
*Deschutes River*

**Christina Stratis Hunt**  Animals/Pets
*Catnap Time*

**Ron J. Suddard**  Nature
*Fall*

**Carol Lynn Givans**  Animals/Pets
*Trip Watching*

**Wanda Vickie Lee Goodfellow**  Animals/Pets
*I Stole Daddy's Chair*

**Lily Yeo**  Nature
*Lone Tulip*

**Christina Danielle Critelli**        Animals/Pets
*Deep Thoughts*

**Belinda Zapatka**        Animals/Pets
*Curious Cow*

**Christine Winefred Symmerman**        Nature
*Flowers And Ladybugs*

**Rick E. Hale**        Nature
*Quiet Earth*

**Mike F. Johnston**        Other
*Waiting For Dawn*

**Janine F. Mitchell**        Nature
*Flower*

**Kathy Alma Wall**                                    Other
*Fading Past*

**Ann Marie Wical**                                    Children
*An Angel's Smile*

**Ritu Akhtar**                                    Animals/Pets
*Wild Beauty*

**Diane Marshall**                                    Nature
*The Beach*

**Vanessa White Bennett**                                    Children
*Here I Come!*

**Vassilis K. Argirakis**                                    Travel
*Ancient Greek Temple Of Poseidon At Sounio*

**Adolfo Esteban Pizarro**                    Animals/Pets
*Whispers—Susurros*

**Yuri Vladimirovich Tselikin**                    Other
*Untitled*

**Marco Margini**                    Nature
*Monet's Waterlily Pond*

**Christopher Mark Jones**                    Children
*The Missionary's Son—Eilat, Israel*

**Jason Samuel Brown**                    Nature
*Texas Sunset*

**David Joseph Podeswik**                    Nature
*Whale Watch*

**Marilyn Fay**           Children
*Little Devil*

**David Mark O'Laney**           Travel
*Krumlov Castle*

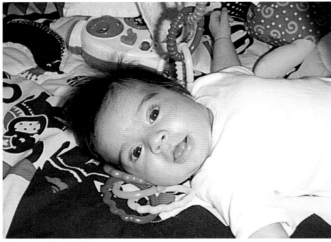

**Allison Centolella**           Children
*Brianna Lynn*

**Audrey Mae Paules**           Animals/Pets
*Bighorn Sheep*

**Carmen De Oliveira Integlia**           Portraiture
*Carmen And Blue Man*

**Jacques Couture**           Animals/Pets
*Baby 016*

**Nikole Carene Schaitel**　　　　　　Children
*Angel*

**Gail Patricia Norman**　　　　　　People
*Nawlins*

**Stacy D. Shuker**　　　　　　Other
*Moss Street Fire*

**Christa L. Plaster**　　　　　　Children
*Waiting For The Great Pumpkin*

**Harry Stratton-Brown**　　　　　　Travel
*Pelicans*

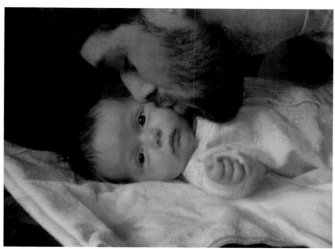

**Lucinda Ann Kimrey**　　　　　　Children
*Special Kiss*

**Patsy M. Gregoire**                                      Nature
*Beauty*

**Eric Antonio Stevenson**                                Portraiture
*An Asian Beauty*

**Jennifer Elizabeth McAlexander**                        Nature
*Cub Lake*

**Lottie P. Doyle**                                       Nature
*Rose Moss*

**Nicholas Simon Hancock**                                Travel
*Big Sky Country*

**Donna J. Kelly**                                        Other
*Shrimp Boats*

**James L. Roberts**                                    Animals/Pets
*Shadow Swimming With Thelma*

**Liz Clements**                                        Animals/Pets
*Mango*

**Elena Barchi**                                        Nature
*The Silence*

**Rodolfo Carvajal**                                    Animals/Pets
*The Sea And The Lion*

**Glenn Kuhlman Fluehr**                                Travel
*Waikiki Beach*

**Brenda Raybion**                                      Children
*Bubbles*

**Nicolas Antonio Jimenez**                    Children
*Up To Something*

**R. Douglas Lemkay**                    Sports
*Pacific Swift*

**Jean E. Gervais**                    Travel
*The Cathedral—Paris*

**David Defiore**                    Animals/Pets
*All Dressed Up And Nowhere To Go*

**David G. Mansfield**                    Travel
*Alum Creek Marina*

**Monica R. Partlow**                    Animals/Pets
*Dogs That Do Damage (For Pictures)*

**Aurora Angelique Rivera**　　　　　　　　Children
*A Day In The Sun*

**Ele Wilde**　　　　　　　　People
*Waiting For A Bemo*

**Kathy L. Suggs**　　　　　　　　Children
*Car Ride*

**Lawrence S. Kozy**　　　　　　　　Nature
*May Your Nets Be Filled*

**Erin C. Sanders**　　　　　　　　Children
*Babyface*

**Penny (Rue) Ellen Morris**　　　　　　　　People
*Untitled*

**Dan John Keelean**                                  Travel
*Changing Of The Guard At Lenin's Tomb, 1991*

**Brian Patrick McDonald**                       Animals/Pets
*Jas And Morris*

**Keri Brook Friedman**                                Other
*Floating*

**Kevin Phillips**                                      Nature
*Fallen Leaf*

**Maarten Simon Nieuwenhuizen**               Travel
*Desert Company*

**Karen Teresa Stephenson**                     Animals/Pets
*Best Friends*

**Karen Jean Baker**
*Michigan's Biggest Fans*

People

**Massimo Zerega**
*Turtle Train*

Animals/Pets

**James W. Sharrock**
*Country Road*

Nature

**Judy Alfan**
*What Are They Looking At?*

Animals/Pets

**Margot Lynn Gordon**
*Emerald Bay, Lake Tahoe*

Nature

**Christina Marie Zeigler**
*Little Sweetie Pie*

Children

**Robert A. Brinley**                                           Nature
*Tennessee Panorama*

**Jeffrey Iliff Wilson**                                        People
*Ghostly Christmas*

**Elizabeth Lynne Edwards**                                     Nature
*Reflections*

**Eva Shou**                                              Animals/Pets
*Lily*

**Karlyn Rita Morissette**                                     People
*Skipping Stones*

**Dennis Mike Correa**                                       Children
*First Birthday*

**Thomas Ray Freeze**    Nature
*Sunshine*

**Uzi Mandel**    Travel
*Children In Thailand*

**Nafi Gurdal Alaeddinoglu**    Nature
*Sunset*

**Lonny Bartholomew**    Nature
*Sunrise In Cabo San Lucas*

**T. J. Steies**    Nature
*Iowa Winter*

**Jennifer B. Reed**    Children
*Mayumie's Surprise*

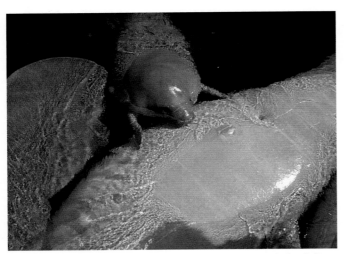

**Pamela Ann Zide**          Animals/Pets
*Baby Manatee*

**Lynn Roebuck**          Nature
*Inner Depths, Quiet Splendor*

**Gauri V. Mohnalkar**          Children
*I Love You*

**Glenn Frederick Marfell**          Humor
*Hiking*

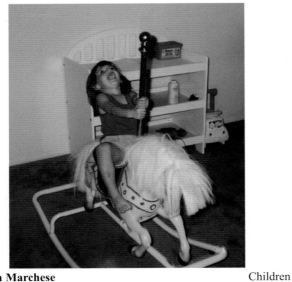

**Loretta Marchese**          Children
*Yee Haw!*

**Rodney Korn**          Nature
*Two Of A Kind*

**Pamela D. Shattuck**                     Children
*Mommy, Look What I Did*

**Richard Timothy Burgess**                Nature
*The Lonely Leaf*

**Donald Eugene Brannam**                  Travel
*Mackinac Island Lighthouse*

**Robert Kevin Allen**                     Children
*Cheeky Jasmine*

**Liza Trang Tran**                        Nature
*Beautiful Winter, Alberta*

**Michael Ely DeSorda**                    Nature
*Monet Forest*

**Cammi L. Campbell**
Nature
*Misty Morning*

**Todd R. Carter**
Children
*Amongst Friends*

**Pamela Jeanne Klein**
People
*Horse Soldier*

**Andrew Edward Ainsworth**
Nature
*Ullswater*

**Jeff Groendyke**
Other
*Man In The Stone*

**Chris A. Hughes**
Nature
*Candy Skies*

**Lyn L. Iglesias**        Animals/Pets
*Potted Maltese*

**Michael Joseph Brody**        Children
*Mirror, Mirror, On The Wall, Who's The Cutest Baby Of Them All?*

**Christina Scagnelli**        Animals/Pets
*My Cat*

**Frie M. Reich**        Children
*There Is My Song, Elmo*

**Duane Palmer**        Nature
*Fire In The Sky*

**Lori Ann Meshew**        Nature
*Red Bluffs*

**Sarah Anne Osborn**        Animals/Pets
*You've Got Mail*

**Gloria Dorothy Smith**        Children
*The Swimmin' Hole*

**Paola J. Silva Canale**        Nature
*Atardecer Frente Al Mar*

**Trudy E. Vella**        Children
*Nola, Five Years Old*

**Nancy Campbell**        People
*The Father I Once Knew*

**Michelle Veracruz**        Travel
*Corpus Sky*

**Wei Kiang Tang**                          Animals/Pets
*Yuki Baby*

**Teresa K. Johnson**                          Nature
*Heading For A Storm*

**Shoji Takahashi**                          Travel
*Washington Monument—Baltimore, MD*

**Anh Thi Ly**                          Nature
*Paradise Flower*

**Gary Joshua Alpert**                          Animals/Pets
*Red-Eyed Tree Frog*

**Sue Scafe**                          Travel
*April In Venice*

**Bruce Geoffrey Yates**                    Children
*Bree, Two*

**Wilson Hodge Hopkins**              Animals/Pets
*Seal Relaxing On Christmas Day*

**Peter Arnold**                                  Travel
*Rocket Returning*

**Jon K. Spaulding**                    Animals/Pets
*Fish*

**Loida C. Lasam**                         Children
*Que Linda!*

**Deborah Valerie Seen**                Portraiture
*The Smarties Boy*

**Marsha M. McDaniel**                              Nature
*Dancing Saguaros*

**Judy Guiao**                                      Sports
*1989 Cafe Racer*

**Deborah H. Moody**                                Children
*Baby Bunny*

**Edward E. Prothero**                              People
*Untitled*

**Deana Miltenberger**                              Children
*Nessa And Daddy*

**James Jon Hailey**                                Animals/Pets
*Flower*

**Maureen Cash** Animals/Pets
*Happy Jake Cash*

**Sally Ann Peterson** Animals/Pets
*I Love Santa*

**Deborah June Schwartz** Nature
*Underground Skyline*

**Eric Roy Anderson** Nature
*Walking Giants*

**Laslo Gabany** Nature
*Fern*

**Michael Anthony Hermogeno** Children
*Ha!*

**Esme** (partially obscured)
*Mar...*

**Marcel Joseph van Dun**                                    Travel
*Winter Sun Over Romo*

**David Andrew Seigler**                                     Nature
*Untitled*

**L. Michael Black**                                         Nature
*Evening Hue*

**Elaine Jean Calvert**                                      Nature
*Old Gardener Holds Her Prize*

**Brent L. Magstadt**                                        Nature
*Northwest Spirits*

**Maria Rita Koenen**                    Animals/Pets
*Rita's Pal Sam*

**Linda I. Carnahan**                    Other
*Pete*

**Don W. Boehler**                       Children
*Jared*

**Danielle Irene Rodriguez**             Animals/Pets
*Stuie*

**Subin Mathew**                         Other
*The Path*

**Gabriela Acosta Peschard**             Animals/Pets
*Simon*

**Mollyanne Ruth Coolidge**                    Children
*Umbrella Kids*

**Ed Kostek**                                        Animals/Pets
*Tigger And Princess*

**Peter Daugulis**                              Animals/Pets
*Our New Sister*

**Miryam Luisa Knutson**                        Children
*I'm Mad, Grama*

**Esperanza Gallego**                    Nature
*Colors Of The Fall*

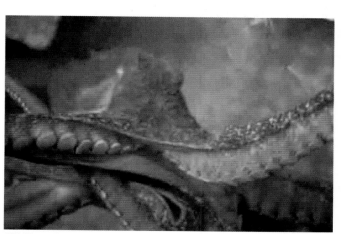

**Eli Zane Owens**                              Animals/Pets
*Octopia*

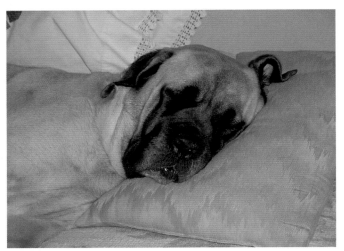

**Andrea D. Mull**  Animals/Pets
*Sleeping Beauty*

**Charity E. Eltagonde**  Children
*Sightseeing With Trudi*

**Cynthia D. Gibson**  Nature
*Moon In The Morning*

**Annaliisa Gillings**  Travel
*Beyond Horizons*

**Abdul Basir Kazi**  Nature
*Rose From Rehana's Garden*

**Cody Brian Sewell**  Animals/Pets
*Cow Sign*

**Kathleen E. Bodie-Johnson**                    Animals/Pets
*Majesty*

**Cecilia Escobar Gómez**                    People
*Mercado*

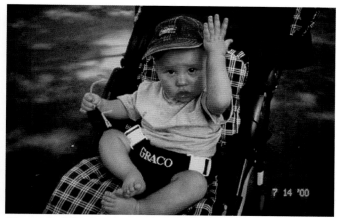

**Sharon Ledfford**                    Children
*What Was I Thinking?*

**Josephine Hyland**                    Animals/Pets
*Proud Dad*

**Karen S. Muisus**                    Nature
*Dionis Beach*

**Rudolf W. Grau**                    Animals/Pets
*Bird*

**Rhonda Hall Allen**                                  Animals/Pets
*Selena In The Spring*

**Efrain Santiago**                                          Other
*Beautiful Flowers*

**Jennifer J. Thompson**                                  Children
*Gone Fishin'*

**Jacke Shipwash**                                          People
*Innocence*

**Elli Rae Steil**                                          Other
*Black-And-White Bricks*

**Susan I. White**                                          Travel
*La Hinch, Ireland—The Rainbow Says Everything!*

**Tommy E. Sisco**          Nature
*Beach Prints*

**Charles Lloyd Turner**          Travel
*London Eye*

**Shelley S. Plakans**          Travel
*Barbados Sunset*

**Steven Michael Sullivan**          Sports
*Hang-Gliding*

**Steven A. Certilman**          Travel
*The Malacòn, Havana*

**Jason Alan McCall**          Nature
*Wonderer*

**Donna Ann O'Neill**                                              Animals/Pets
*My Duckie!*

**Billy Ray Moore Jr.**                                                  Travel
*Okinawa*

**Simara Lozada**                                                      Nature
*Storm*

**Dominique Deschênes**                                               Action
*Flower*

**Melissa Richards**                                                 Children
*Dress-Up*

**Alex Shain**                                                    Animals/Pets
*Bird*

**Lisa L. Eklund**    Children
*Sweeties*

**Joanne Hentschel**    Children
*Sleeping Buddies*

**Jeff L. Fowler**    Nature
*Bird*

**M. Suzi Speiser**    Children
*Tender Moment Between Child And Pet*

**Lisa Bagshaw**    Children
*Lunchtime!*

**Shannon Kathleen Anson**    Animals/Pets
*Close To Giraffe*

**Andy Ryan Taylor**                                    Animals/Pets
*Turtle Love*

**Christina Marie Smith**                                    Other
*Snow Men*

**A. T. Nagy**                                    Nature
*Spider In Waiting*

**Devyn Marie Weinstein**                                    Animals/Pets
*I Think I'm Gonna Be Sick*

**Judie Patricia Holm**                                    Travel
*Mountain Glacier*

**Panagiotis Intakidis**                                    Travel
*Art Stone*

**Bianca Henrea Armbrister**
*Storyteller Of The Ren Fair*

People

**Masayo Yamashita**
*The Stonehenge*

Travel

**Twila René Skidmore**
*Naptime*

Children

**Chuck Dowling**
*Man's Best Friend*

Portraiture

**Stacy Lyn Cox**
*White Sands Visit*

Other

**Jennifer Claire Robinson**
*Lily Pads*

Nature

**John J. Tyson** Children
*Precious Moments*

**Nancy and Ted Matlock** Nature
*Fall Splendor*

**Klaas Verhoef** People
*Love*

**Kathy Lynne McDaniel** Animals/Pets
*Naptime*

**Donna L. Wells** Other
*Docked*

**Shelley Jean Alger** Nature
*The Last Dawn Of The Century*

**Marylene Joan Williams**　　　　　　　Animals/Pets
*Have A Great Day*

**Patricia D. Robles**　　　　　　　Children
*A Walk On The Beach*

**Phyllis Joann Russell**　　　　　　　Nature
*Man In Field*

**Heather Ann Frey**　　　　　　　People
*Glassblower*

**Joan Louise Petty**　　　　　　　Travel
*Mandolin Player In Venice*

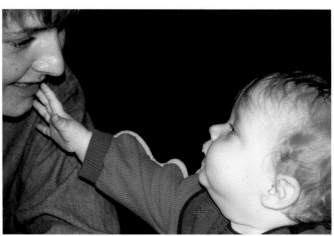

**Torben Hedegaard**　　　　　　　Portraiture
*My Mother*

**Slobodanka P. Filipovska**                                    Action
*Megi I Marko*

**Shane Ayres**                                    Nature
*Castle Ruins*

**Gerd Bräutigam**                                    Portraiture
*Chris, The Berlin Boy Of '99*

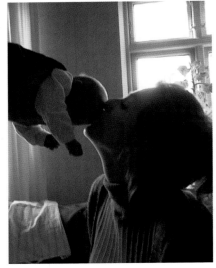

**Lars Christensen**                                    People
*Mother And Baby*

**Kent Robert Didion**                                    Animals/Pets
*Watermelon Good!*

**Sue M. Woomer**                                    Nature
*Goodnight, Sweetheart*

**Einar Gunnlaugsson**                    Nature
*By The Snæfells Glacier In Iceland*

**Rene Guerrero**                    Other
*Music—Guitar*

**Bellamy Benedetto Budiman**                    Nature
*Forest Sunset*

**Ashley Michelle Gleason**                    Animals/Pets
*Lazy Kitty*

**Barbara J. Frederick**                    Nature
*Fall On The River*

**Richard S. Gillogly**                    Action
*Replenishment For Peace*

**Jolene Esther Johnson**  Children
*Friends*

**Guillermo Martínez Caballero**  People
*Dance On The Air*

**Melissa Gayle Parrish**  Other
*Gift From Above*

**Raluca Mitrea**  Travel
*Jump Up Soca Fest (Big Truck)*

**Betty Lou Cochran**  Children
*Emily*

**Tina Marie Hedin**  Animals/Pets
*Lions*

**Nicole Suzanne Furtaw**                Children
*Daddy And Me*

**Marlene Mary Brown**                Animals/Pets
*Twins Or Mirrored Image?*

**Lori Okinaga**                People
*The Hunt For Summer*

**Shalee Marie Vance**                Children
*I'm Gonna Get Those Wascally Wabbits!*

**Bonnie Dawne Evaschuk**                Animals/Pets
*Back On The Chain Gang*

**Edward J. Paddock**                Travel
*Schloss Blankenhain Castle In Germany*

**Francis Michael Unson**
*Isla Vista Sunset*
Nature

**Sebastian Mariusz Kasinski**
*Style Is Everything*
Children

**Deborah Kay Miller**
*Perfect Petunia*
Nature

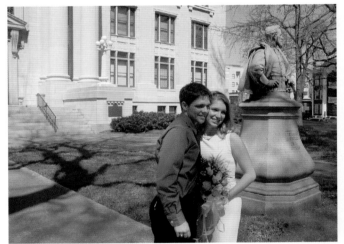

**Wendy Joy Guider**
*The Perfect Day*
People

**Jeri Lee Jacks**
*Sunset Over Trouville Pond*
Nature

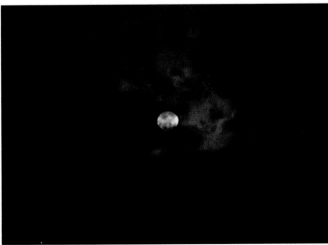

**Sharon Lee Woodlief**
*Storm Of Full Moon Faces*
Nature

**Kris McWhinnie**                                      Portraiture
*Me*

**Odilys Paula**                                            People
*Boys On A Donkey*

**James Richard Battista**                              Other
*Kinzua Bridge, 301 Feet High*

**Philippe A. Cashaback**                            Nature
*Northern Exposure*

**Viktor Palm**                                              Travel
*Fascination Of The Mountains*

**Linda Lorine Twyman**                            Children
*Dr. Katie*

**Dave Nacht**                    Nature
*Ebbett's Pass Sunset—Tahoe, Nevada*

**Eran Gilat**                    Other
*Old*

**Glenn A. Morin**                Nature
*Bird Of Paradise, Mexico*

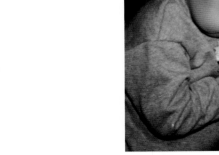

**Leslie Denise Vestal**          Children
*I Can Smell It!*

**Bohdan Tkaczyk**                Nature
*Storm Over Grand Marais*

**Claudia Rathbun**               Children
*April And Autumn In December*

**Mary Taglieri**                    Nature
*You Go Your Way; I'll Go Mine*

**Justin Scott Baer**                    Nature
*Through The Trickle Of Time*

**Elizabeth Anne Moore**                    Nature
*Sunset At Lake Yosemite, California*

**Sandra Lou St. Denis**                    Animals/Pets
*My Penny In A Box*

**Brian K. Saindon**                    Nature
*Piddle Paddle*

**Allyson Martin**                    People
*Grandma's Kiss*

*141*

**Frank J. Bruno Jr.**   Nature
*Snow Barn*

**Rakesh M. Pathak**   Travel
*Historic Monument*

**Leona L. Everhart**   Nature
*Serenity*

**Mysia Lyn Wolfe**   Animals/Pets
*Smiling Beluga*

**Donnie Carl Shipman**   Animals/Pets
*Whazzup?*

**Sandra K. Gaston**   Children
*Brotherly Love For Now*

**Michael Robinson Moon**  Travel
*Strawberry Fields*

**Ilario M. Zanardo**  Other
*Something Is Burning Or Is Up In Smoke*

**Donald P. Copeland**  Travel
*Prague*

**Jean Ann Crowe**  Other
*Prairie Wind*

**Garth Andrew LeFort**  Nature
*Cloudy Mountain*

**Lori J. Phillips**  Nature
*Cancùn Sunrise*

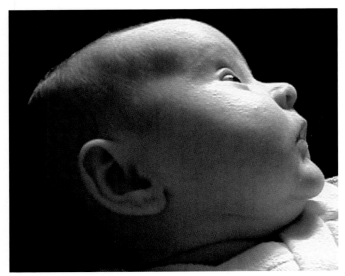

**Kimberly Ann Schratwieser**      Portraiture
*Artistic Shot Of Nicky*

**Brian Lee Burchfield**      Animals/Pets
*Watching The Races*

**Eberle Jane Morgan**      Children
*Gathering Love*

**Christopher Edward Henson**      People
*Mom Working*

**Shaun Laws**      Travel
*Scattering Pigeons—Kathmandu, Nepal*

**Jean-Jacques Cricoveanu**      Nature
*Flower Of The Dune*

**Rhonda L. Holland**  Animals/Pets
*I Have Mail!*

**Diana Lynn Walton**  Nature
*To God Be The Glory*

**Dixon William Keller**  People
*Pride*

**Mirko Rizman**  Action
*Reflection*

**Rebecca Rose Östergren**  Travel
*A Summer's Evening In Stockholm*

**Bill Frantzis**  Animals/Pets
*Bird Love*

**Anne Line Stordiau** Nature
*Zoom*

**Rosemary Gwladys Clarke** Animals/Pets
*My Polo Pony*

**Terri Gentile** Other
*Sunset*

**Ron Knerem** Nature
*On The Way*

**Cruceru I. Dorin** Children
*Petru*

**Christopher Pablo Francisco Cornejo** Nature
*Princess Amongst Others*

**Croydon L. Kemp**                    Nature
*Arrival*

**Kathy J. Smith**                    Humor
*Angel Baby?*

**Matthew Grimble**                    Travel
*Ford Truck*

**Jason John Mahoney**                    Nature
*Rainbow Through The Korean War Monument*

**Jan Cary**                    Nature
*Organ Mountains Snow*

**Cheryl Fawn Winnie**                    Children
*Little Princess*

**Paola Amadei**                                      People
*Triste Trópico*

**Elly Filov**                                        Other
*Red Bicycle*

**Deborah Jean Vuicich**                        Animals/Pets
*Waiting For Lunch*

**Paloma Sanchez Torres**                             Other
*Relax*

**Abdalla Ibrahim El-Hilo**                        Children
*Mohd*

**Ronald Allan Parks**                               Sports
*Ready To Rumble*

**Susan Ellen Mitcheltree**                    Children
*Molly And Payton*

**Louie Schoeman**                    Travel
*Green Within Pompei Ruins*

**Bunny R. Krupa**                    Children
*Baby Bunny*

**Andrew Ramon Padilla**                    Travel
*Rain In Rome*

**Paul E. Thébeau**                    Nature
*Evening Serenity*

**Robin F. Russak**                    Animals/Pets
*Goofy Christmas Alphaboo!*

**Yee Weng-Tao Vivit**                    Animals/Pets
*Meow*

**Patricia Gene Tracy**                    People
*A Day At The Zoo*

**Heidi Soeborg**                    Animals/Pets
*Spring Is In The Air*

**Geert Sonck**                    Nature
*The Bridge*

**Ted Lazich**                    Nature
*Clouds*

**Alvin G. Kaumeyer**                    Animals/Pets
*Pondering*

**LaVerne Odom Holman**    Animals/Pets
*Pepper, My Fat Cat*

**Kathleen Andersen**    Nature
*Morning Reflections*

**Janine Frances Shelton**    Animals/Pets
*Peanut*

**Stacia Moore**    Travel
*Storm Over Masonic Mine*

**Randell Lee Midkiff**    Nature
*Reflections*

**Sergey A. Demyanenko**    Humor
*Beggars*

**Dana D. Sorrell**                    Nature
*No Vacancy*

**James D. Thomas**                    Nature
*Park Lake In The Fog*

**Michael Eldon VanLent**              Travel
*Ohio River*

**Alex Nevin**                         Other
*My Old Shoes*

**Darren John Cepulis**                Children
*Quetzal*

**Cheryl A. Hendrix**                  Nature
*Creek*

**Amy Marie McGinnis**
*Blossoms Of Love*

Nature

**Kelli S. Kessler**
*Serious Strike*

Other

**Sharon K. Stewart**
*Rock-A-Bye Baby*

Children

**Debby Shelton**
*Tranquility*

Nature

**James Bernard Humburg**
*Offering You A Coke And A Smile*

Other

**Elizabeth M. Chartier**
*Swan Lake*

Animals/Pets

**Herbert Reppard McMahon**  Nature
*Tughill Sunrise*

**Daljinder Singh**  Nature
*Cactus Flowers At Big Bend National Park*

**Valerie Elaine Provencio**  Nature
*Long Day Into Night*

**Josephine Carter**  Nature
*Ahhh*

**Bartek Kotkowski**  Nature
*Ski Tour*

**Heath Ryan Sharp**  Other
*War And Glory*

**Eve Arnold**                                          Animals/Pets
*Deer In The Fall*

**James Whitaker**                                           Nature
*Forest Pond*

**Veronica Priscilla Corral**                               People
*Untitled*

**Shannon K. Lebeuf**                                      Children
*Mandy In The Daisies*

**Theresa E. DeLuca**                                        People
*My Girls*

**Lora Rae Anderson-Egan**                              Animals/Pets
*Love Birds*

**Austin Garnett Voyer**                                    Nature
*Desert Tortoise*

**Brienne N. Mayer**                                        Nature
*Dawning*

**Norma J. Shannon**                                 Animals/Pets
*Morning Coffee*

**Brian R. Reed**                                           Other
*Portrait*

**Jeff Charles Cealey**                                     Other
*Lamp*

**Brandy Elizabeth Mangum**                                Travel
*Himba Hut*

**Christie Noelle Arellano**  Animals/Pets
*Christmas? I'm Thrilled!*

**Roger Wesley Nafziger**  Travel
*St. Croix*

**Lisa Linkmeyer**  Nature
*Leopard*

**Debbie Ann Nelson**  Children
*Sweet Pea*

**Sandra Ann Kritner**  Children
*New Arrival*

**Philip Thomas Farquharson**  Animals/Pets
*California Gray Fox*

**Rose K. Ondrajka**  Animals/Pets
*So Cute*

**Linda J. Parker**  Nature
*Feeding Frenzy In Paradise*

**José Augusto Alves**  Other
*Alhambra*

**Teri V. Clem**  Nature
*Gnarley Tree, 1999, Lunar Moon*

**Chris R. Gray**  Animals/Pets
*Reflection Of One*

**Richard Joseph Wilson**  Nature
*Three Turtles*

**Denise Marianne Mercuri** People
*Baby-Sitting's A Hard Job*

**Samantha J. Marshall-Scales** Children
*How Do Ya Get Out Of Here?*

**Merrill Bedford Davis** Animals/Pets
*Seiko The Watchdog*

**Patti Jann Deibert** Animals/Pets
*The Christmas Horse*

**Stephen Lyle Demarest** Nature
*Sailing On An English Lake*

**Anne Sheehan** Children
*Siblings*

**Mamerto Amores Irasga**
People
*Fish Of Mine*

**David Matthew Verhagen**
Nature
*Mount Robson*

**Linda Mary MacLean**
Children
*Beautiful Britt*

**Alyssa Colleen McKinney**
Animals/Pets
*Reading The News*

**Kohei Tai**
Other
*Sydney Opera House*

**Andrea Lyn Walthall**
Travel
*St. Charles Bridge*

**Emily Ann Haas**                    Animals/Pets
*Star*

**Dawn Louise Dille**                    Children
*The Conversation*

**Evelyn Falto**                    Animals/Pets
*My First Bike*

**Mary Frances Herron**                    Children
*Amber*

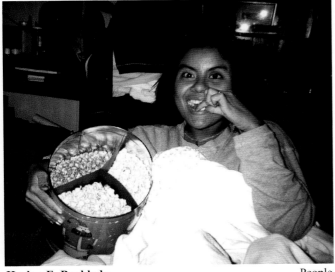

**Harlan E. Buchholz**                    People
*Popcorn*

**Suzi Schor**                    Animals/Pets
*I Am The Cat, You Are The Help!*

**Celia Vieira Tunes**                    Children
*Brazilian Soccer*

**Kirsten Elizabeth VanderWall**          Children
*The Kiss*

**Martha Ann Hilliker**                   Other
*Placing The Historical Texas Star*

**Robin Lyn Moody**                       Travel
*Self-Portrait*

**Sindy Jean Juliano**                    Nature
*Into The Abyss*

**James Mathew Chappell**                 Other
*Ribbon Of Winter*

**David L. Blakley**                                                    Nature
*Kyrgyzstani Autumn*

**Lotus Yip Sanders**                                                  Action
*World Record Dive*

**Amber J. Rumph**                                                     Travel
*Beautiful Sunrise*

**James Stephen Murray**                                               Humor
*Office Standoff*

**Robert DeZinna**                                                     Nature
*Springtime*

**Teresa A. Costarella**                                         Animals/Pets
*Killer Pit Bull*

**Debbie C. Bonshire**                    Animals/Pets
*Toilet Paper, Please*

**Riny Van Abel**                    Other
*Fountain*

**Andrew Harrison Maloney**                    Travel
*New York Skyline*

**Mauro Mirandoli**                    Nature
*Montagna*

**Andy H. Maloney**                    Travel
*Liberty At Dusk*

**Christian Laroche**                    Travel
*World Trade Center, New York*

**Mirjam Letsch** People
*Bhopi, A Singer On The Desert Of Rajsthan, India*

**Deborah Sioux Thompson** Animals/Pets
*Echo's Eye*

**Ed Riles** Nature
*Colorado's Continental Divide*

**Brett Thomas Futral** People
*Seaside*

**Tanya L. Chard** Other
*Hope*

**Donna May Madge** Nature
*Northern Lights*

**Laura A. Packer**                    Nature
*Smokey Mountain Majesty*

**Jon Leonard McDonald**                    Animals/Pets
*Weatherford Cow Dawg*

**Franklin L. Miller**                    Other
*Jet*

**Jason W. Hoyle**                    Other
*A Split Second*

**John Clare Shearer**                    Nature
*Land's End*

**Walter Anderson Keaton Jr.**                    Nature
*Bee Takes A Break*

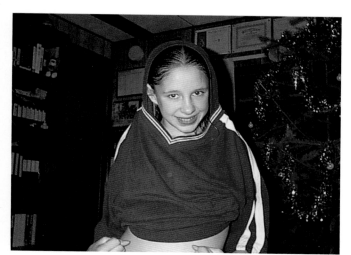

**Darrel R. Hammack**     People
*Nikki*

**Keena L. McIntyre**     Children
*Alaskan Grown*

**James Alan Mello**     Animals/Pets
*Googly Eyes*

**Daniel L. Fegel**     People
*On The Job*

**Peggy Lawrey**     Nature
*Arkansas River Sunset*

**Mary C. McKiel**     Nature
*Iona's Gift*

**Wanda B. Foell**                                              Other
*These Feet Are Tired—This Is Home For Now*

**Tessa A. Wyman**                                              Children
*Little Fishies*

**Natasha Fay Lahey**                                           Children
*Madelyn*

**Michael Lane**                                                Nature
*Mountain Tree*

**Gordon Eugene Miller**                                        Children
*Grandchild With Hat*

**Latricia Lynne Fulkerson**                                    Nature
*New Mexican Sunset*

**Elizabeth Anne Monroe**                    Nature
*Natural Fence*

**Darryn Brooks**                    Nature
*Ripple Effect*

**Ken S. Miller**                    Sports
*Silent Flight*

**Milind Hari Mustikar**                    Children
*My Family*

**Jane Tintner-Bishop**                    Animals/Pets
*Cracker Reading The Daily Comics*

**Damian Murray Lord**                    Animals/Pets
*My Best Friend*

**James D. McDonie**                    Animals/Pets
*Squirrel With Corn*

**Denise Lynne Cruz**                    Travel
*The North Shore On Oahu*

**Chammy Lo**                    Nature
*A Look A Day In L. A.*

**Trista Marie Douglass**                    Animals/Pets
*Scarlet O'Hairy*

**Kathleen Ann Molhan**                    Children
*Must Be Baseball Season*

**Fábio Luciano Vieira**                    Nature
*Sea*

**Jennifer Nicole Callaway**     Children
*Kassiepoo*

**David Allen Sierk**     Nature
*The Beauty Of The Snow*

**Polly DeMott**     Nature
*Stormy*

**Jesse Allen Levengood Jr.**     Other
*Weathered Memory*

**Rebecca C. Mak**     Children
*Joy*

**Amer Maher Meknas**     Nature
*A Comet!*

**Julius Valsson** Portraiture
*Óli KR*

**Julius Vincze** Nature
*Fisherman's Sunrise, Japan*

**Melissa J. Kornicki** Animals/Pets
*While You Were Away . . .*

**Adrienne Nell Doherty** Children
*I Wonder . . .*

**Steve Ashley Fidgeon** Other
*The Hall*

**Sergio Betancourt** Humor
*Well I Am Hungry!*

**Sal Chavez** Sports
*California Beach Skate Sailing*

**Jason Douglas Thornsberry** Nature
*Greenville Falls*

**Roy A. Holland** Nature
*High Water*

**Elaine Nowell** Animals/Pets
*Lady And The Tramp*

**Delaine Dunaway Mullins** Children
*Precious Moment*

**Robert Edward Bloom** Nature
*Butterflies*

**Geraldine M. Guerin**                    Animals/Pets
*Just Watching*

**Merideth Leslie Berkovich**                    Other
*Who Is Checking Who Out!*

**Mylaine Marie Waring**                    Travel
*An Evening In Florida*

**Kim Sage Difederico**                    People
*Gotcha*

**Jason Eric Straatmann**                    Other
*Old Drum*

**Jesse James Church**                    Portraiture
*Reflections Of The Past*

**Patricia A. Walters** Nature
*Nature, My Snowy Woods*

**Milton Bruce Gillie** Children
*Little Lady In Red*

**Eric R. Parson** Children
*Briant*

**Robert Gene Jutras** Nature
*Tranquility*

**Melissa Kay Stone** Children
*Koren's Fountain Fun*

**Nelson Christopher Harvey** Travel
*Port Lookout*

**Frances Joyce Gower**                                    People
*Treasured Memories Of My Great-Grandparents*

**Leigh S. Austin**                                    Animals/Pets
*Yorkie Love*

**Madonna Combs Powell**                                    Other
*Jessica And The Great Outdoors*

**Gyula Oláh**                                    Children
*My Little Boy For My Thirty-Ninth Birthday*

**Fred Sherman Salter Jr.**                                    Nature
*Underwater World*

**David John Gibbons**                                    Action
*Narrow Escape*

**Phirun Roeun**
*Nevada Mountain*
Nature

**Katrina Lorraine Boley**
*Truth*
People

**Tina Marie Austin**
*Fly*
Children

**Kim Kristine Kemp**
*Other Uses For A Rubber Ball*
Children

**Ellen S. McBride**
*Miss Jordyn*
Children

**Guy Andrew Paddock**
*National Cathedral, Washington D.C.*
Travel

*177*

**Joe House**     Animals/Pets
*Hungry Bird*

**Heather Ellen Heinks**     Animals/Pets
*Princess Peanut*

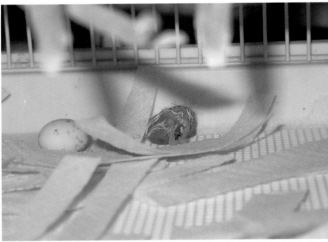

**Bob J. Bassetti**     Animals/Pets
*New Kids On The Block*

**Debra Lynn Baker**     Children
*Beautiful Danielle*

**Thurlow Charles Farnsworth**     Nature
*Hale Bopp*

**Sarah Elizabeth Newby**     People
*Only In Mexico*

**Joyce Gabriel Kaishar**  Children
*Rosey Cheeks*

**Betty L. Dwyer**  Animals/Pets
*Samantha And Paul*

**Jordan Kyle Barclay**  Portraiture
*Trance*

**Verna Mary Stahl**  Nature
*Mt. McKinley*

**Marissa Rene Crane**  Nature
*My Heaven*

**John Kurt Dudley**  Nature
*Great Look*

**Andjelko Glivar**
Children
*Real Baby*

**Kelly J. Clark**
Other
*Old Truck*

**Teri Jo Shoemaker**
Animals/Pets
*A Face Only A Mother Could Love*

**William Alfred Ferrarini**
Nature
*Connecticut Lakes, New Hampshire—God's Country*

**Donna-Michelle Young**
Nature
*On The Bayou*

**Dave J. Mathias**
Nature
*Virgin Winter Stream*

**Sunshine J. Bennett**                    Nature
*Tibochina*

**Mathew Dane Conner**                    Animals/Pets
*Wonder And Amazement*

**Michaél C. Tallant**                    Animals/Pets
*The Eyes Have It*

**Jeraud Barbut**                    People
*Affar On Lac Assal, 1981*

**Kelley James Langford**                    Animals/Pets
*Just Hangin' Around*

**Eric Yuzon**                    Travel
*The Westin Courtyard In A Mexican Desert*

**Robert Gerald Batey**                    Animals/Pets
*The Pirate*

**Mary Renee Sevek**                    Children
*Quiet Time*

**Richard D. Fischett**                    Other
*Small Town Snow*

**James Timothy Kinsey**                    Animals/Pets
*Oh, Pretty!  Oops, Wet!*

**Rolan Edward Logan**                    Nature
*Steps To Spring Cherry Tree*

**Brookzscat A. Brooks**                    Animals/Pets
*Brookzs Cat House, Home Of Elegant Maine Coon Cats*

**Sara Beth White**  Nature
*Nature's Perfect Rose*

**Colleen M. Berg**  Animals/Pets
*Sad Eyes*

**Howard John Oswalt**  Children
*John And Melissa*

**Ginger Sizemore**  Animals/Pets
*Mom, Look What I Found*

**Robert B. Kolar Jr.**  Nature
*Spirit Cave*

**Sharon Ann Richert**  Travel
*Sailing And Sunrise*

**Wanda Faye Hindmon**                    Animals/Pets
*Smokey On The Couch*

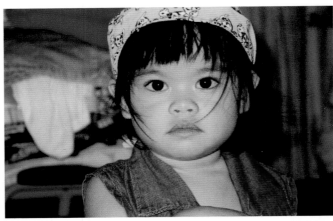

**Levana Capon**                    Children
*Amazing Kate-Lior*

**Daniel Otto Salin**                    Nature
*Frozen Fog On The Boise River*

**Nadean Dawn DeBeaucamp**                    Children
*Surprise*

**Alan Brian Kraus**                    Travel
*Shooting Pool*

**Sandra Jane Bowman**                    Nature
*Mallard Duck*

**Raymond George Ross** Nature
*Rocks*

**Jane L. Arrowsmith** Children
*John Meets New Baby Sister For The First Time*

**Suzanne Joyce Dahlman** Nature
*Sunset On The Ranch*

**Dawn M. Wyzard** Nature
*My Coy Boy*

**Cheryl Ann Strong** Animals/Pets
*Pretty Kitty*

**Jeffrey Park Jones** Nature
*Amazing Tree*

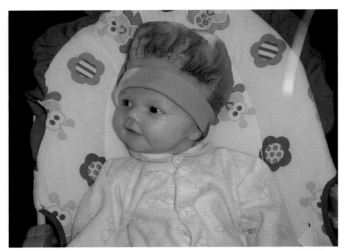

**Peter M. Bolewicz**                                   Children
*Baby Casmira*

**Beverly Ann Sportelli**                                   Nature
*Raging Sun*

**Cindy Sullivan**                                   Animals/Pets
*Red-Tailed Hawk*

**Julia Mainwaring-Berry**                                   Nature
*God's Palette*

**Joyce Rae Cunningham**                                   Animals/Pets
*Computer Cat*

**Jennifer Dodd**                                   Animals/Pets
*Bama's Nose*

**Jong Ha Lee**                    People
*My Pretty Daughter*

**Kristie Lynn Appugliese**                    Children
*Too Tired To Eat*

**Trina L. Frick**                    Children
*A Little Something From Santa*

**Tyler Dennis King**                    Other
*Another One Marks The Wall*

**John Joseph Von Hegel**                    Other
*Sunset*

**Allyson Buchta**                    Animals/Pets
*Perfect*

*187*

**Geneva Lee Manke**                    Children
*Real Cowboy*

**Roy Douglas Cosby**                    Nature
*Barrier Island*

**Katherine Anne Perry**                    Other
*Guardian At Walter Street Cemetery*

**Amelia Kathryn Wagoner**                    Nature
*Plant In The Rocks*

**Robert B. Shipley**                    Children
*Gotcha*

**Berith M. I. Larsson**                    People
*Black And Red*

**Diana Leigh Zeller**　　　　　　　　Children
*I Want That One, And That One, And That One . . .*

**Jenny Crosby**　　　　　　　　Travel
*Meteora*

**Richard Wade Calkins**　　　　　　　　Children
*Real Butterfly Kisses*

**Amanda Latha Lemieux**　　　　　　　　Animals/Pets
*My Romeo*

**Yoshio Endoh**　　　　　　　　Animals/Pets
*Mein Lieber Billy*

**David Arther Daley**　　　　　　　　People
*Lions' Coach And My Granddaughter*

**Peter Sutter**
*Young Ladies*

Portraiture

**Linda Sue Wells**
*Fudgesicle Baby*

Children

**Paul Thompson**
*In Thought*

People

**Vikram Karumbaiah**
*Liberty*

Travel

**Henry Dulak**
*One Day Bouquet*

Nature

**Denise E. Bergsma**
*Day Is Done*

Nature

**Gail Tileston**        Animals/Pets
*Really, My Cat Ate My Homework*

**Robert Charles Foultz**        Children
*So There!*

**Cynthia Annette Cox-Grollman**        Other
*Remembrance, Beauty, And Sorrow*

**Cynthia Burkhardt**        Animals/Pets
*Cat-titude*

**Carolyn C. Hancock**        Children
*Fabulous Bubbles*

**Saima Asim Siddiqui**        Children
*Ha Ha Ha*

**Ardy Langord** — Children
*That Was Some Cake!*

**Natalie Rivera** — Children
*Sophia's First Bikini*

**Teresa Susan Wilkinson** — Nature
*Flyaway Seeds*

**Nelson Lee Wilson** — Children
*My Sweet Grandbabies*

**Robert Joe Ailstock** — People
*In The Good Ol' Days*

**Robert Lauren Lightsey** — People
*Oscar*

**Lisa Marie Eberhart**                                     Children
*My Best Friend*

**Steve Mellor**                                     Nature
*Waterspout*

**Darlene Martin**                                     Children
*Don't Touch*

**Lisa Burns**                                     Children
*Outside Looking In*

**Jamie L. Genovese**                                     Animals/Pets
*My Girly Girls*

**Catherine Restivo**                                     Travel
*Goat For Sale*

**George R. Mikhail**          Other
*Underwater*

**Ray Alexander**          Animals/Pets
*Sleeping With Daddy*

**Margaret A. Maes**          Sports
*Safe At Home*

**Barry K. Adams**          Sports
*Slide*

**Lori Anne Zimmer**          Animals/Pets
*First Swim*

**Philip Alan Zangari**          Animals/Pets
*Here Comes The Sun*

**Larry G. St. Clair**　　　　　　　　Travel
*Memorial Day—Wrightsville Beach, NC, 2000*

**Kathryn Ann Pavlish**　　　　　　　People
*Reflections On A Bus*

**Miles Doran**　　　　　　　　Action
*Blue Angels*

**Michael Thomas Hendricks**　　　　　Travel
*Trucker's Flower*

**Deborah Wray Jolly**　　　　　　　People
*Rest At The Rio Grande*

**Cheryl L. Michelfelder**　　　　　Animals/Pets
*Meet Stinker*

**Graeme Trevor Fordham**                    Nature
*Last Summer*

**Shervin Salsali**                    Nature
*My Camera's Getting Wet!*

**Andrew J. Wilcox**                    Animals/Pets
*How'd He Get In There?*

**Joan Kathryn Paulino**                    Nature
*Evening Cruise*

**Mark Robert Lowther**                    Nature
*Sailor's Delight*

**Dorothy Jean Palmer**                    Animals/Pets
*Precious And JR Playing*

**George William Kahl**          Nature
*Morning Bud*

**Willem Dieleman**          Nature
*Birdhouse*

**Camille Jade Cousins**          Nature
*A Kapas Island View*

**Tara Ann Williams**          Animals/Pets
*Bug The Cat*

**Adrienne Lisa Taylor**          Children
*Zach's Reflection*

**Rodney Little**          Other
*The Love Of Christ*

**Brett Leich**                                      Children
*I Don't Want To Leave*

**Liew Yeu Hing**                                      Other
*KLCC Twin Towers*

**Cathy Suzanne Rash**                                      Children
*Marilyn Who?*

**Jerry G. Kemp**                                      Nature
*Morning Feathers*

**Sherrill Montgomery**                                      Animals/Pets
*Bear And Lucy*

**John C. Block**                                      Children
*Luke's First Day Of School*

**Monty Britton**      Children
*The Last Emperor Of My Family Tree*

**Travis Paul Mitchell**      Nature
*Streaming Sky*

**Herlien Tan**      Action
*Fireworks*

**Andre Teixeira**      Children
*Long Way*

**Danielle Clayre Mowers**      Portraiture
*Train Stop*

**Darren Malphurs**      Children
*I'm Tired*

**Kevin Ray Navarre**　　　　　　Animals/Pets
*Hungry Wolf*

**Karla J. Larson**　　　　　　Humor
*Fooling The Neighbors*

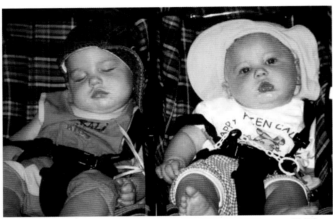

**Alessia Ciuchi**　　　　　　Children
*Twins*

**Vicki DeMiero**　　　　　　Animals/Pets
*First Snowfall*

**Carmelo C. Montalbo**　　　　　　Other
*A Farmhouse*

**Dewey Douglas Sanders**　　　　　　Animals/Pets
*Okay, Everybody Smile*

**Cohara Hossepian**                    Animals/Pets
*Piccolo*

**Rusty Hines**                    Nature
*Majestic Mt. McKinley*

**James A. Hobkirk**                    Nature
*Orange Hibiscus*

**Kendric Wayne Johnson**                    Animals/Pets
*Iguanas On Girl's Arms*

**Evan Simon Jacobs**                    Animals/Pets
*A Photogenic Camel*

**Kris Simones**                    People
*Chillin'*

**John Espinosa**    People
*Stunned*

**Diana Sue Pagni**    Children
*Friends For Life*

**Andrew Michael Pierpoint**    Nature
*High Sky*

**Nathan Wandrey**    Travel
*Panoramic View*

**Joe B. Carballo**    Humor
*Tongue-tings Wrong*

**Mary-Louise Warren**    Animals/Pets
*Poncho Villa Begging*

**Joseph J. Tuti**                                        Sports
*Prestwick Bell*

**Katie Allison Grams**                                  Nature
*Sunshine On A Cloudy Day*

**Linda L. Kupstas**                        Animals/Pets
*The Swans*

**Joni Mari Maniatis**                      Animals/Pets
*Duck*

**Marty C. Edwards**                              People
*A Rhyme With No Reason*

**Michael David Davies**                    Animals/Pets
*Two Bears*

**Roger A. Michalski**      Other
*Old Barn*

**Robin M. Nolte**      Animals/Pets
*I Have Had Such A Hard Day!*

**Doreen Rix Meeker**      Animals/Pets
*Old Blue Eyes*

**Amanda Cathleen Garland**      Nature
*Amanda's Tree*

**Mark S. Schroeder**      Animals/Pets
*Duck Tail!*

**Greg Carl Korner**      Animals/Pets
*Osprey*

**Curt M. Herman**                                                      Nature
*Snow*

**Kathy L. Thompson**                                                   People
*Wish Upon A Sunflower*

**Loretta Root**                                                        Nature
*Antelope Canyon*

**Christina Michelle January**                                          Children
*Fragrance Of Spring*

**Eric Nierstedt**                                                      Nature
*Sun Time*

**Rana M. Buckner**                                                     Animals/Pets
*Between Man And Beast*

**Todd Steven Ricketts**                                    Animals/Pets
*Morgan Territory*

**Charles Manahan**                                         People
*Grandpa's Seventieth Birthday*

**DeAnna L. Oden**                                          Children
*Brotherly Love*

**JoAnn Julie Findley**                                     Children
*Tanna*

**Susan E. Love**                                           Nature
*Pot Of Gold*

**Veronica Sofia Tiliander**                                Children
*Every Bubble In The World For You, Mum*

**Glenn Richard Towler**     Travel
*Clear Tunnel*

**Wanda D. Summar**     Nature
*Globe Flowers*

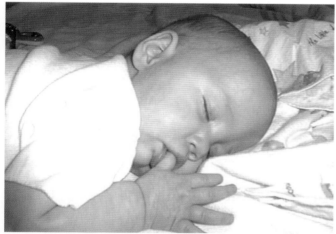

**Cathy Annette Jay**     Children
*Nana's Girl*

**Juliette Anne Coolidge**     Nature
*Winter Peace*

**Patrick John Chanley**     Animals/Pets
*Fawn*

**Cynthia T. Herrin**     Children
*Picking Flowers*

**Shirley L. Bailes**        Nature
*Sunrise*

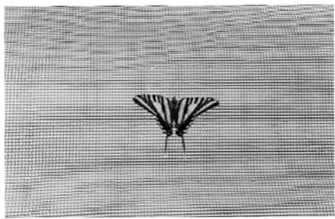

**Marie Laverne Nopola**        Animals/Pets
*Butterfly On Screen*

**Chris Benson**        Children
*No Hooks?*

**Kimberly Ann Streelman**        Animals/Pets
*Sandy*

**Mireya L. Hooten**        Nature
*Welcome To Alaska*

**Tina M. Howe**        Children
*Tuckered Out*

**Patricia Lynn Mann**                    Travel
*Bali*

**Emma Beatrice Arnold**                    Other
*The Kiss*

**Tiffany Erin Chapman**                    Children
*Kameron*

**Sharon Kaye Moore**                    Children
*On The Farm*

**Jan Bryant**                    Portraiture
*Queen Kristina*

**Arnold B. Baking**                    Travel
*Pristine . . . Almost*

**Lucina Radd**                    Nature
*I'm So Pretty! Oh, So Pretty!*

**Mark H. Waller**                    Nature
*Easter Tulip*

**Edward C. Darby**                    Animals/Pets
*Day At The Lake*

**Wayne Cathey**                    Travel
*Koblenz, Germany—Meeting Of The Rhine And Mosel River Monument*

**Stella Bernadette Oliver**                    Animals/Pets
*Sylvester & Sylvester*

**Michael Lewis**                    Travel
*Kathmandu Holy Men*

**Ruth Ann Fuoss**                                   Animals/Pets
*Our Room*

**Norman Williams**                      Children
*Kiss From A Friend*

**Cristy Joe Hughes**                      Children
*Flower In The Flowers*

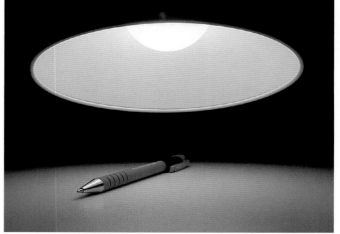

**Jesse Steven Schmidt**                 Other
*Pentrait*

**Amy Elizabeth Tvaroha**               Nature
*Mingus Mountain*

**Sandra Ann Fernando**               Animals/Pets
*Let Me Drive You Crazy*

**Dawn Flanagan**                    Animals/Pets
*Got Water?*

**Jamie Renee Pastorelli**                    Nature
*End Of The Earth*

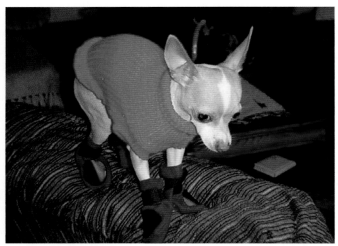

**Ron H. Martinmaki**                    Animals/Pets
*Okay, Take 'Em Off Now!*

**Darlene Ruth Rice**                    Nature
*Cape Hatteras, NC, Sunrise*

**Michael Duane Wahl**                    Travel
*Liberty Splash*

**Lara Lynn Ford**                    Children
*Bluebonnet Innocence*

**Theresa Marie Burrous**                                    Nature
*Sunset At Laguna Beach*

**Shannon Ivy Colon**                                    Nature
*Colors Of Sunset*

**Steve Eydelman**                                    Travel
*The Building*

**Patricia Leanne Vargas**                                    Children
*Close-up*

**Beverly Kendra Ragsdale**                    Animals/Pets
*Pole Cat*

**Molly Rebecca Westlake**                                    Children
*Mirror Image*

**Chris Fricke**                                                    Humor
*My Best Friend, Mr. Glass*

**Missy J. Miller**                                                 People
*What Do I Do With These Things?*

**Jill Rachelle Tarket**                                       Animals/Pets
*Squished*

**Mary Helen Hicks**                                                Nature
*Reflections At Sunset*

**Kim P. Weaver**                                                   Nature
*Big Sur Cypress Frame*

**Chrissy Dawn DeSantiago**                                       Children
*Baptism*

**Holly Malia**                                    Portraiture
*Joslynn*

**Lena Klassen**                                   Animals/Pets
*Waiting For Spring*

**Mark Robinson**                                  Other
*Special Operations*

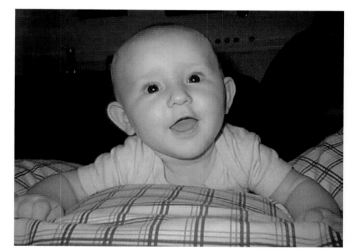

**Leah Andrea Rutherford**                         Children
*Hello, Beautiful!*

**Jason John Stainbrook**                          Portraiture
*Side-By-Side*

**Janice Lenore Engle**                            Travel
*Walt Disney World*

**Jessica Perry**                                    Children
*This Is My Angel Cat!*

**Jeannine McKinney**                          Animals/Pets
*Cleopatra Goes Horse Camping*

**Jerrie Lynn Dean**                                    Other
*A Warm And Peaceful Evening*

**Pam Jean Steele**                          Animals/Pets
*New Life*

**Alessandro Cattelino**                          Portraiture
*Thought*

**Karen Leigh Woys**                                    People
*Make A Wish*

**Timothy Alexander Rogers**　　　　　　Children
*Bradley's Adventure*

**Lisa Lynn Czerw**　　　　　　Animals/Pets
*Jelly Beans*

**Shela LaVelle Davis**　　　　　　Children
*Texas Baby*

**Glenn Daniel Konrady**　　　　　　Animals/Pets
*Honkers Squabbling*

**Heather Marie Johnson**　　　　　　Children
*Innocence*

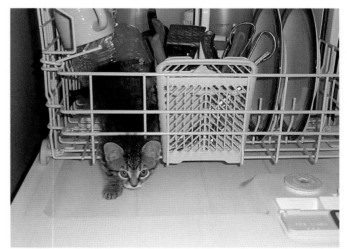

**Diane Johnston**　　　　　　Animals/Pets
*Busted*

**Kay Hemmick** People
*Baptism*

**Kemberley Frayer** Nature
*Sunset*

**Jessica A. Thornton** Children
*Pumpkin Patch*

**Cyril Gnanaprakasham** Other
*The Final Abode*

**Chris Anderson** Children
*That Was Fun!*

**Frederick Albert Medina** Animals/Pets
*Young Seagull Of Plymouth*

**Rhonda Lou Pierce**  Nature
*Redneck Riviera*

**Elizabeth Rodriguez**  Humor
*Help!  A Monster!*

**Stan Armstrong**  Travel
*My New Boat . . . The Little One*

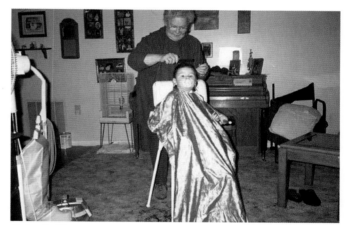

**CeLeste Shaver**  Children
*First Haircut*

**Tara Lee Gilbreath**  Children
*Bunny Love!*

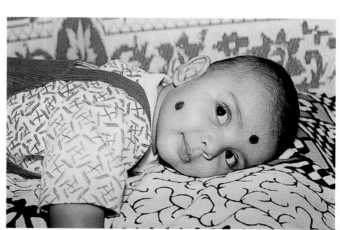

**Kiran Kameswar Anivilla**  Children
*Don't Worry, Be Happy, Keep Smiling*

**Galina Lyssenko**                               Other
*Untitled*

**Eileen Daphne Tyrrell**                         Nature
*Peace Rose No. 2*

**Belinda Sue McAlpine**                          Nature
*Where Heaven And Earth Meet*

**Nathalie Carole India Vitiello**                Animals/Pets
*Peaceful Greek Cat*

**Karl W. Hammerberg**                            Humor
*The Readers*

**Ajey A. Tatake**                                Animals/Pets
*Swan Lake*

**Jeanne Snyder** Children
*Snowhood*

**Crystal Archer Williams** Nature
*Tulips In Bloom*

**Mary Hollingsworth** Children
*Watch Out, Hollywood*

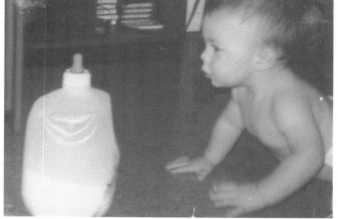

**Roger E. Banfield** Children
*Josh And His Jug*

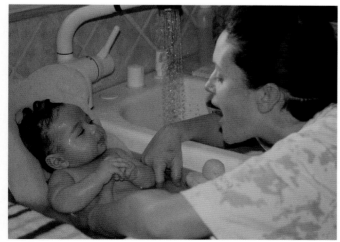

**Ed Miller** Children
*Adoration Accepted*

**Marija Kruhek** Nature
*The Hairy Little Jimsing, A Wonder Of Nature*

**Dawn Marie Peters**      Nature
*Sunset*

**Christina Yvette Perez**      Nature
*Wahkeena Falls*

**Kristi Anne Gossman**      Animals/Pets
*Max In A Basket*

**Corrie Linda Lee Ahrens**      Animals/Pets
*Cuddling Kitties*

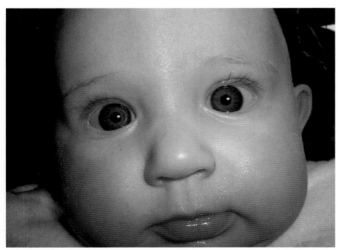

**Gary Poole**      People
*Jess*

**Ruth Meshriy**      Nature
*Sabbath Sunrise*

**Apache Vivian**        Children
*First Day Of Baseball*

**Bea M. Newman**        Children
*Grammie's Angel*

**Sarah Jane Phillis**        Nature
*Ghost Horse*

**Sherry K. Metzger**        Nature
*Fall Sky*

**Greta F. Bernard**        Children
*Granny's Girl*

**Debra M. Galiardi**        Nature
*Peace*

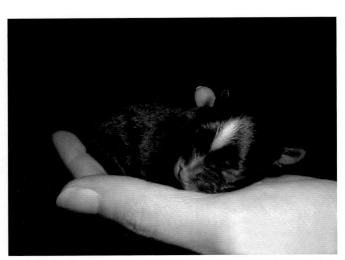

**Patricia L. Patrick**                    Animals/Pets
*First-Born Puppy*

**Linda M. Lauer**                    Animals/Pets
*Friends*

**Beth Howlett**                    Animals/Pets
*Seagull*

**Sherri L. Abdel-Majid**                    Animals/Pets
*Christmas Is For Cats, Too!*

**Cassandra Leigh Vance**                    Children
*Fifty-Two Pickup, Anyone?*

**Terry V. Reeves**                    Children
*Grandma's First Love*

**Virginia Carmel Spradlin**                    Nature
*Grist Mill At Ciris McCormick Farms In Virginia*

**April Marie Michalski**                    People
*Easter 2001*

**Rupert Guarina Enriquez**                    Nature
*Morning Green*

**Monica D. Miller**                    Children
*Captured Innocence*

**Anni Phillips Worster**                    Portraiture
*I'm A Believer*

**Michelle D. Comingore**                    Nature
*Puzzle Perfect*

**Bruce H. Baretz**             Animals/Pets
*Cool In The Pool*

**Sharon Squires**             Other
*Father And Son*

**Andre Sermer**             Children
*Naomi At The Fence*

**Erik S. Finwall**             Nature
*Bryce Canyon*

**Matt Dyche**             Nature
*The White Friend*

**Lynn Crisci**             Animals/Pets
*The Watcher*

**Scott D. Titus**　　　　　　　　　　　　　　Children
*Warm And Quiet*

**Novabiana Indradjaja**　　　　　　　　　　　Other
*Small World At Night*

**Larry Edward Straits**　　　　　　　Animals/Pets
*Molly's Friend*

**Era Vuksani**　　　　　　　　　　　Animals/Pets
*Squirrel*

**Kevin Bruce Lamke**　　　　　　　　　　　Nature
*Goshen Sunset*

**Brian Michael Zahorodniuk**　　　　　　　Nature
*Wish I Was Still Here*

**Randy Koh**                                        Animals/Pets
*Big Eyes*

**Chris Perry**                                              Nature
*Northern New England Fall Color*

**Melissa Ellen Davis**                              Animals/Pets
*Woolly Bully*

**Wendy Anne Bamford**                                       People
*True Love's Kiss*

**Prasad K. Krishnan**                                    Children
*I'm Watching!*

**Alicia Jo McMahan**                                   Portraiture
*Samuel*

**Tammy Marie Soiseth**        Children
*First Love*

**Liliana Patiño**        Travel
*Monk Without A Head*

**Darlene J. Rasmussen**        Nature
*The Old Dead Tree*

**Carol Ann Campbell**        Humor
*The Ole Soft Shoe*

**Francoise Suzanne Marga**        Travel
*La Foule Illuminee By B. Laures—Montreal*

**Saleh Ahmad Mohamad Al Ustad**        Portraiture
*Divorce*

**Maria do Socorro C. C. B. Vasconcelos**          Children
*Girlfriends*

**Twyla Dawn Braatz**          Animals/Pets
*Life's Real Treasures*

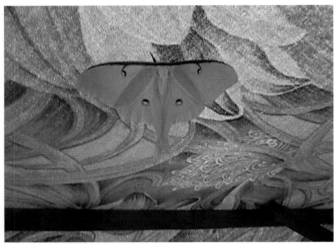

**Jennifer Robin Marshall**          Nature
*Metamorphosis*

**Veronica Vargas**          Animals/Pets
*Kosmo*

**Kathrine Raelyn Rend**          People
*Communicating Before Entering*

**Karen M. Cappello**          Nature
*An Autumn Stroll*

**Carol S. Rozzi**                              Animals/Pets
*Backyard Wildlife*

**Marian A. Mihalcik**                          Animals/Pets
*I'm Precious*

**Jomar J. Enciso**                             Other
*Reflections*

**Marian A. Mihalcik**                          Animals/Pets
*Did You Call?*

**Ange Hawkey**                                 Nature
*Lilac-Breasted Roller*

**Lori J. Brooks**                              Nature
*Tropical Plant*

**Tiffany April Sefa**    Nature
*Whisper*

**Ashley Nicole Schwerin**    Animals/Pets
*Brand-New*

**Sheila Cole**    Children
*What A Baby*

**Vicky L. Snider**    Nature
*My Winter*

**Jo-Ann M. McGovern**    Other
*Tranquility*

**Annette Smith Hinson**    Children
*Playtime Or Mealtime?*

**Betsy Maisel**                                                    Nature
*Morning Magnolia*

**Carey R. Cook**                                                   Children
*Gotcha This Time!*

**Marilyn J. Adams**                                                Children
*Whispers*

**Thomas Michael Taylor**                                           Portraiture
*All In Fun*

**Clarissa Rene McCallum**                                          Humor
*The Kiss*

**Martina Simms-Hilbert**                                           Children
*Afternoon In The Petrified Forest*

**Sarah B. Dunham**  Nature
*Mountainous Beauty*

**Robert Joseph Ketner**  Nature
*Monterey Cypress*

**Anita LaForte**  Nature
*My Home In Springtime*

**Joseph William Gitto**  Children
*Here's Looking At You, Kids!*

**Jan Merrill Richardson**  Animals/Pets
*Squirrel Fig Leaf*

**Margareth Giskeødegård**  Nature
*The Sunrise Over The Mountain*

**Brandy Lynn Grummons**                    Children
*Heather In The Sandbox—May 1998*

**Kay Frances Binzer**                    Children
*Popsicle Tongues!*

**Kazuko Honda**                    Children
*La Poupée*

**Ronald D. Edfors**                    Nature
*Mississippi River Lock In Winter*

**Stephen Anthony Jubb**                    Nature
*Carmelia*

**Jeffrey L. Oakes**                    Children
*Happiness Is . . .*

**Mark Steven Smith**                                    Nature
*Sunset*

**Julie Ann McNair**                                  Animals/Pets
*First Impressions*

**Fahim Ahmed Razzaque**                                 Travel
*Rocky Mountain Dreaming*

**Kiwi Ng**                                              Other
*Street*

**Roo du'Jardin**                                        Nature
*Mycena*

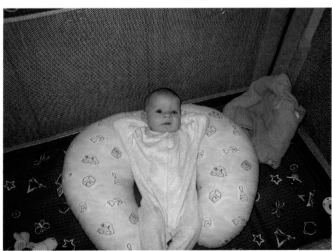

**Margaret Ann Priest**                                Children
*Just Lounging Around*

**Nik Watt**        Animals/Pets
*Alfie*

**Robert H. Meserve**        Nature
*New England Birches*

**Kathleen E. Carlton**        Nature
*View Of The Storm*

**Albert Guillermo**        Travel
*On A Good Day*

**Karina Hartmann Adamsen**        Portraiture
*Eyes*

**Nig Salamis**        Portraiture
*The Tunnel*

**Mike W. Shields** Nature
*Mother Nature's Air Show*

**Marsha Smith** Animals/Pets
*My Baby*

**Charles Edward Lemons** Children
*Bobby At The Beach*

**Michal Pikus** Travel
*Hawaii*

**Diana Irene Ferrero** Nature
*On The Other Side*

**Susan Marie Snyder** Nature
*Sunset Fisherman*

**Alfonso Vitela**  Nature
*Serenity*

**Nancy Wong Yan Hwa**  Nature
*Heaven's Light*

**Jennifer Sue Powell**  Travel
*The Continental Divide*

**Lara Elizabeth Bee**  Animals/Pets
*Teri's Idea Of A Good Napping Buddy*

**Heather Rene' King**  Nature
*Daisy*

# ARTISTS' PROFILES

**ABEL, RINY VAN**
This picture was taken by a Dutch castle, Paleis Het Loo. We were showing our American friend around. She was over here for three weeks and enjoyed it all very much. She is from Phillips, WI.

**ACOSTA PESCHARD, GABRIELA**
Simon has given me and my family so many beautiful moments of love and friendship that I do really and truly believe that there's a very big soul behind his eyes. Thanks so much, Simon.

**ALAEDDINOGLU, NAFI GURDAL**
Every second implies a change in our world. I have been photographing sunsets to capture and, if possible, to share with others such changes brought about by the sun. Ankara, the city where I live, makes this task easier with its air pollution. I am a scientist (currently a professor in microbiology) who has hobbies. You name it, I'll tell you; mostly with sudden changes of mind! In my youth, I did manage to make some pocket money out of photography.

**ALEXANDER, RAY**
I love my cats! Roman, the black one, and Dante, the tabby, are brothers. They were found in a dumpster at two days old. I had to handfeed them. They are about ten weeks old in this photo. At three-and-a-half and sixteen pounds each, they still love to sleep with Daddy.

**ALLEN, ROBERT KEVIN**
I was downloading photos to my computer when Jasmine, my three-year-old granddaughter, came into my study. I changed my camera to capture her and shot this photo. I was very happy with it and wanted to share it with the world. My wife, Rhonda, and I live in Bentley, a suburb of Perth, Western Australia.

**ANDERSEN, KATHLEEN**
As a mother of nine children, I welcome the peacefulness of the new day. Mornings are the best time to reflect on the day's events. As I awoke one September morning, I looked out my window and captured the beauty of the new day. What a great way to start a soon-to-be busy day.

**ANDERSON, ERIC ROY**
I took this photo only after viewing the cacti from all angles. As I came around the back of it, it suddenly seemed to be walking away. Living in Arizona, one can never tire of the beauty of its surroundings. From the Grand Canyon and lush ponderosa pine forests to the Sonoran Desert, it truly is a land of continual wonder.

**ANDERSON-EGAN, LORA RAE**
Lora Anderson-Egan is a rural instrumental music teacher in South Dakota. She has always had an interest in photography and minored in mass communications while majoring in music education at South Dakota State University in Brookings, SD. This photograph was taken outside of her apartment one morning while going out to do some errands. There was a whole flock of these birds outside on the electric wires. She took a moment to grab her camera and took some snapshots.

There were some really fun photos, but this is one of her favorite photos out of all she has ever taken.

**ANGUIZOLA, ROGELIO ALBERTO**
Many nights I would stay up for hours waiting for the lightning to start during the 1990 electrical storm season in Guadalajara, Jalisco (Mexico). I was able to take many photographs such as "God's Finger."

**ANUDTARAPANYA, VICHAI**
This photo is a reflection of a memory and an idea. I like to look at everything in its old style, while some people don't like to look at things in that way. This picture also reflects the contrast between the growth and imbalance of society. "Lives" represents the simple way of life of some Thai people. There is not any colorfulness of life or new technology; everything is natural and has per se beauty as a work of art. This photograph is my first entry in this contest.

**ARELLANO, CHRISTIE NOELLE**
This is a photo of my five-year-old cocker spaniel, Maggie. She is like a daughter to me and my husband, Tino, and like a sister to our sons, Gage and Donavin. I love taking pictures of her because of her funny droopy expressions. I very much wanted a Christmas picture of her and was just thrilled to capture this shot! We all love her very much and are blessed to have her as a member of our family.

**AUSTIN, TINA MARIE**
This is a photo of my niece, Emily. I don't get the opportunity to go home and visit very often, so when I do go home, I make sure I bring my camera. My nieces and nephews grow so fast, and I am not there to see it. In taking their pictures, I feel like I can capture little precious moments of their lives and, from a distance, witness them grow.

**AYRES, SHANE**
I am seventeen years old and lucky enough to live near some of England's finest countryside. My main interest is films and filmmaking. I currently attend film school in Sheffield, which is our nearest city. This photograph was taken on my last visit to our local wildlife park, which is situated on the grounds of these ruins. Unfortunately the animals have been relocated to various other parks and zoos, as it is now closed.

**B. GUIER, ALICE**
The blue sky and white statue together that day created a photo opportunity I just couldn't pass up. Sam Houston is located on I-45 just south of Huntsville, TX. I am a beginner at photography and travel around Texas quite a bit so I have plenty of subject material for photos. I have a non-commercial website, www.abguier.8m.com, where you can view some of my other photos.

**BAER, JUSTIN SCOTT**
Close your eyes for a moment. Imagine a place to which you would escape, a place of comfort, a place where when you open your eyes, you find yourself encircled by enchantment, the very middle of nature's own. This photo was taken in the Cascades, the place where I like to go and wonder,

surrounded by lush trees and wild waterfalls, a place many will never see. That is why I took this picture, "Through The Trickle Of Time," so I could share it with the rest of the world.

**BARCLAY, JORDAN KYLE**
This photo is my attempt to capture the essence of darkness in Ryan's lyrics. It was taken during a group photo shoot of the band 1369. The image was accomplished by the use of proper angles of two different light sources. I enjoy using black and colored lighting for the object and the background. The style of my photography is similar to art I create with illustrations, paintings, and computer art. I have a hobby in manipulating my photography with my original artwork in photoshop and illustrator. This original photo was later stylized to fit the CD booklet composition.

**BERKOVICH, MERIDETH LESLIE**
I have always enjoyed photography. My favorite subjects are people and animals. In this shot, I have combined them both with my husband, Bob, and my thirteen-month-old blue roan paint Filly, Tia Eva Meria. To capture a moment on film, it has to be candid and unplanned. It just has to happen. I will treasure this moment forever because I happened to capture it on my camera. I guess I could have captioned this, "Give me a kiss, or I will eat your hat!"

**BERNARDI, SUZANNE LINN**
I am the manager of the cardiac catheterization laboratory at our local hospital. I have been in the medical field for twenty-five years. My husband gave me a digital camera for Christmas, and this was my first major picture-taking event. This is my granddaughter, Makenna, at her first birthday party. She loves to wear hats.

**BETANCOURT, SERGIO**
I try to bring my digital camera with me at all times, looking for that special photo. I caught my son, Sergio E., fooling around with the burgers, trying to tell me, "Well, I Am Hungry." I am a computer technician.

**BLAKE, GRACE**
My first trip to London was an eye-opening experience . . . and much of it was viewed through the eye of my camera. I was especially taken with Hyde Park, a beautiful, tranquil place in the midst of the bustling city. That is where I happened upon this comical row of gulls, calming and sunning themselves without a care in the world. I love to travel. Captured moments like this become treasured memories.

**BLAKLEY, DAVID L.**
This is a photo of golden poplar trees on the western side of Lake Issyk-Kul, Kyrgyzstan. It was taken with a Canon A-1 35mm with a 28mm wide angle lens at F5.6 and 250th/sec. I frequently traveled to the former USSR while working as a U.S. Department of State security contractor from 1993–1999. I am a 1978 graduate of Highland High School in Highland, KS, and give my Lord Jesus all the glory for my photography skills.

**BRAATZ, TWYLA DAWN**
I enjoy taking pictures of my family when they are

busy doing other things and don't notice my camera in hand. Here is a picture of my husband with his little buddy, Obi, one of our four standard poodles. My husband is watching television, and Obi is watching everything.

**BRANDON, HOLLY NICHOLE**
This is a photo of my seven-and-a-half week old chocolate Lab named Moose. I was trying very desperately to get a good picture of him to email friends and family, and he refused to sit still. After numerous bad photos, I finally gave up and sat down in the grass. As he was running to pounce on me, I snapped this shot. Every time I look at this photo, it makes me smile because it reminds me of how rewarding animals are. No matter what my day brings, I know when I get home he'll be running for me with unconditional love.

**BRINLEY, ROBERT A.**
This mountain panorama was taken while my wife and I were on vacation during Thanksgiving of 2000. We were driving through the Cade's Cove area of Smokey Mountain National Park when we came across this beautiful landscape. This picture was taken with a digital camera that takes panorama style photographs. This photo is actually four pictures digitally stitched together to make one panorama.

**BRITTON, MONTY**
East meets West; that's the literal truth in this case. His name is Marvin. His father is American and his mother is Chinese. Daddy speaks to him in English, and Mommy speaks to him in Mandarin. At eighteen months old, Marvin has already been to China. This photo catches Marvin enjoying his Great-Uncle Byron's "palace" in Canada. Marvin has one set of grandparents in the United States and one set of grandparents in China. He is the only grandchild for both grandparents. That's why we look at Marvin as "The Last Emperor Of Our Family Tree."

**BROOKS, LORI J.**
I'm dedicating this photograph in memory of my father, Robert. I owe my artistic eye to him, a photographer and an artisan himself. It seems like most of my entire life, I've had a camera or an artist's paintbrush in my hands, always ready to capture the ordinary and the extraordinary. This photo was taken at the New York Botanical Gardens in their conservatory. The plant is in the family Ericaceae and is called macleania coccoloboides. It is endemic to only Ecuador and nowhere else. I also like to incorporate my photos into my artwork, where I specialize in painting landscapes, fairies, and dragons.

**BROWN, MARLENE MARY**
Our family has been going camping in Pennsylvania for over ten years. We often take pictures while visiting the Amish Country. These twins were just standing at the fence on the side of the road, probably watching traffic go by. Taking pictures is a great hobby we enjoy.

**BRUNO, FRANK J., JR.**
When I was a boy, my mother's father gave me a Kodak Brownie camera and told me to "Fill 'er up." I would take the camera on school and family trips and try to accomplish what he asked. My grandfather would go over the developed pictures and make suggestions as to lighting, exposure, and composition, always saying, "A photographer's job is to capture what everyone sees but misses." He is always encouraging and pointing out, "Take as many as you like; one will catch your eye." Over the years, my cameras have changed but Gramps' advice remains true today—"Fill 'er up, one will catch your eye."

**BRYANT, JAN**
The subject of this photograph is statuesque (5'11") Kristina Maley, fresh from the shower, sans makeup, and donning a towel. Her classic features and unique head adornment created an image in my mind's eye reminiscent of ancient Egyptian nobility, hence the title "Queen Kristina." Photography is truly a simple and pure art form!

**BUCKWALTER, JASON**
Living in southern Florida presents many opportunities for great photography, and I never leave home without a camera. This photo was taken on one of my many trips to the Florida Keys. Located halfway between Miami and Key West, Islamorada is a village of islands where a laid-back atmosphere is a way of life. This photo captures the feeling of the Florida Keys and is one of my favorites. I have traveled across the U.S. and thoroughly enjoy the beautiful scenery each state has to offer. To see more of this great country, please visit www.virtualizard.com.

**BURCHFIELD, BRIAN LEE**
Scottie was proudly owned by Brian and Nancy Burchfield. He was our energy, laughter, and love. Scottie was a four-year-old half samoyed half hybrid wolf, but in our eyes he was a gentle giant. This overgrown puppy was constantly looking for new adventure. Scottie loved his owners and would often talk to us with a howl. Sadly, in June of 2001 we lost our loving dog in a tragic accident. Scottie, we love and miss you dearly and there's a missing piece in our hearts with you now gone. We miss you so much, big guy.

**BURKE, JENNIFER**
This is a photo of my two children, Kyle, who is six years old, and Kaylee, who is eight months in this photo. They both like to pose for pictures. I'm always taking pictures of my family. I love sharing photos with family and friends.

**BURKHARDT, CYNTHIA**
I titled this photo "Cat-titude" because I think it sums up the entire existence—unique and enigmatic. There is no other personality and attitude like a cat's. It's written all over their faces, but you just aren't ever sure of what you're reading!

**BURROUS, THERESA MARIE**
I enjoy photographing Mother Nature during her most serene moments. This late October sunset caught my eye, and I was lucky enough to capture it. If I could have included the sound of the surf and the gentle cry of the seabirds with the photo, it would have been perfect!

**BURTON, KAREN**
I really can only take the credit for knowing how to use a camera and seeing a good photograph when there is one. These horses happen to be down the road from a close friend's home. We took a ride one evening and found them to be two of the friendliest horses I've ever been near. It was clearly one of those moments where you are at the right place at the right time. Oh, and of course I happened to be lucky enough to have my camera.

**BUTCHER, LISA MARIE**
This photo was taken on New Year's Day 2001 on Bondi Beach, Sydney, Australia. This beach is really beautiful with its white sand and big waves. I was glad to leave winter behind in New York and thoroughly enjoyed celebrating New Year's in Australia's summer sun. I wanted to capture something of the moment, and the red and yellow of the lifeguard's uniform and equipment were really striking in contrast to the blue, green, and white of the sky, water, and sand. Many thanks to the diligent lifeguards for keeping an eye on the summer surf to ensure we had a safe and fun vacation!

**CABALLERO, GUILLERMO MARTÍNEZ**
My photo was taken during a festival in the center of the city. I like to capture all things that we can't see easily because I think there are many silences in the memory of the world that we can't find in front of the eyes of time. I live in Mexico City and am thirty-three years old. I studied photography in my country in Ansel Adams' school. My complete name is Guillermo Mario Martinez Caballero.

**CALVERT, ELAINE JEAN**
The old woman lives a few blocks away down the street. Her yard was a wreck. Every time I drove by I speculated that she had been ill because the garden was once glorious. So, curious, I stopped one rainy day when she was out tending her beauties. Though bent and faded in body, her grace brought sunshine to the dreary day. She showed me her beauties—showed them all to me I thought—then reached into the shoulder-high weeds and pulled out this perfect prize!

**CAMBARERI, GAIL**
I took this picture of my brother, Anthony, in 1978 just about a month before his life was tragically cut short by another person. He was taken away only two months shy of his nineteenth birthday. I miss him dearly each and every day of my life and I'm so glad I had the presence of mind to take this last picture of him. He was a wonderful, kind person who was loved by many people. This is my tribute to him because to me and everyone who loved him, he will forever be our "Teen Angel."

**CAMPBELL, CAROL ANN**
I've always enjoyed going to Philadelphia to see the Liberty Bell, but this time taking the photo of the bell turned out to be humorous when a little girl walked behind it. She stopped at just the right spot when I snapped the picture. Doesn't it look like she's wearing the Bell as a costume? It looked really cute to me.

**CARLTON, KATHLEEN E.**
This was taken during our New Year's snowstorm. I happened to like the way the icicle hung from the lamp. It was taken at about 6:00 A.M., and it was still snowing. This was a one-in-a-million photo for me!

**CARTER, TODD R.**
This is a photo of my two-year-old daughter after a long hard day at Animal Kingdom in Orlando, FL. She wanted to see the stuffed animals, so her big brother put her right in the middle of all the animals. She snuggled up to one of them, and I couldn't resist taking the picture. In her world, these animals are real, so being able to snuggle up to one was incredible to her.

**CATHEY, WAYNE**
While on a tour of Germany, we stopped at this monument in Koblenz. It was late in the day and ready to storm. I ran off the bus and took this picture and another, then ran back to the bus just before the rain came.

**CATTELINO, ALESSANDRO**
I'm an amateur photographer and have been following this pursuit for five years. I have learned various techniques from famous photographers and have tried to learn how to capture and convey an atmosphere or sensation through the imagination. I prefer photographing landscapes and open spaces. In particular, I enjoy using zoom lenses to capture details in unusual lighting conditions. I mainly use 120-120mm lenses and color dials to get better perspective and color contrast. I also enjoy digital elaboration and use photoshop to create suggestive and imaginative work.

**CEPULIS, DARREN JOHN**
A "Quetzal" is the national bird of Guatemala. It is also the term used for their national monetary unit, and it is how much I paid the father of this little girl to be able to snap her photo on the road to HueHue in Guatemala. This photo speaks to me of the arbitrary value that we often place on our most precious things. My personal motto is this: attention to intention.

**CHAI, TONI-LYNNE WILLKOM**
This photograph is dedicated to my grandfather, William A. Willkom Sr. It was taken a couple of months before he passed away. I hope that through this publication his memory will live on in the minds and hearts of all his friends and family, especially his wife, Damiana, his children, grandchildren, and great-grandchildren. I loved him dearly and always will. I will never forget the times when he and my grandma would take care of my sister and me. I know he loved the art of photography, and so this is for you, Grandpa!

**CHAMBERS, LARRY**
Oftentimes we overlook the beauty that can be found in our own backyard. I live in a small town outside Memphis and have passed this scene for years. But on this day, it jumped out at me, and I had to save it. The Mississippi is so full of power and beauty and affords so many photo opportunities.

**CHAVEZ, SAL**
This photograph captures a magic moment of skate sailing at sunset along southern California's Los Angeles Beach bicycle path. It portrays best the thrill of harnessing the power of the wind while skate sailing. As the wind picks up in the late afternoon, parts of the bike path clear out for us. This turned out to be an ideal time to take pictures for our website www.skatesails.com, and we were delighted with the outcome. While this particular shot was taken off the coast of Playa Del Rey, CA, there are many other bike paths we have yet to discover.

**CHRISTOPHE, WENDY L.**
Here in the south, it is not uncommon for a black cloud to creep up on a spring day. On this particular Easter Sunday, a storm brewed and stirred up twelve different tornados in the area. As the rain stopped and the wind calmed down, the sun peeked through and gave this spectacular cloud such vivid colors of orange with a soft blue sky behind it. The shape of the cloud was fascinating to me, also revealing the end of a violent storm and the beginning of a clear and peaceful evening to come.

**CLARKE, ROSEMARY GWLADYS**
The photograph titled "My Polo Pony" is of my niece atop her favorite pony, taken early one autumn morning after she had been out for a ride. My brother and his family live in a part of South Africa not usually visited by tourists, but which we believe to be one of the country's most beautiful—the Kwa Zulu Natal Midlands. It is also "horse" country with polo being a popular activity amongst the country folk. My interest in photography was not very great until about two years ago when I came to appreciate the beauty of life, purchased a modern SLR camera, and realized that to capture the moment on film is to preserve it forever. My husband and I both belong to the local camera club and spend many happy hours with fellow amateur photographers.

**CLEM, TERI V.**
This photo was taken from Windy Point on Mt. Lemmon in December 1999. I find myself taking drives up to Mt. Lemmon to get away from it all. I moved to Tucson from Alexandria, VA, in 1979 and am now a desert rat. I have a respect for the desert and its wildlife, so much so that I'd rather vacation in Arizona than anywhere else. There's always something new to discover in Arizona, and if it's to be found, I'll find it!

**COLE, SHEILA**
This photo is of my sweet little girl, Amber. I had taken her and her brother, Aaron, out of town on a trip. In our motel room she was just coming out of the bathroom from having her bath, and I surprised her. I snapped the camera just when she screamed. I have always enjoyed looking and sharing this photo with family and friends.

**COOK, CAREY R.**
This picture was taken over twenty years ago of our children, Caleb and Sara. From the time Sara was able to crawl, Caleb would plop himself down on top of her horsey-back style. One day the table turned, and we caught this rare

moment on film. Just as I focused the camera, Sara's little arms with pointed fingers flew upward and she let out a big "yeah," as if to proclaim her victory; I was able to capture it all in time. Sara is now a college student, and Caleb is a marine corps sergeant.

**COOLIDGE, JULIETTE ANNE**
This photograph was taken while on a trip to Wyoming, where my husband and I were engaged. When I looked out over the river, I thought about how peaceful and beautiful it was. I wanted to be able to take the beauty home, so I snapped a few pictures. Now every time I look at this photo I am reminded of the natural beauty my husband and I were able to enjoy.

**COOLIDGE, MOLLYANNE RUTH**
Katraena, four years old, and Tesslyn, seven years old, enjoy their new baby sister, Ariel, three months old, making up for the long wait on her arrival. Every chance they got, they cuddled her, changed her diapers, and even dressed her. This is one of the moments caught where they were being themselves and enjoying each other. I've often attempted to enter photo contests during college, where I earned an associates degree. I have three children and am an administrative assistant for AVCP RHA in Bethel, AK.

**CORAM, CANDACE**
I carry a camera with me at all times with hopes of capturing life at its best on film.

**CORREA, DENNIS MIKE**
The picture I submitted is of my wife's and my first grandchild, Alec Michael. His first birthday was March 9, 2001. He's the son of our daughter, Nancy, and her husband, Joe. We babysit him frequently, and he keeps us running and in stitches all day long. He's a riot, and we love him dearly. His other grandparents, Doug and Judy, are crazy about him and watch him as often as we do. Judy and my wife, Sarah, enjoy swapping stories of Alec's antics.

**COSTARELLA, TERESA A.**
This is a photo of my son's dog, Tasha, with his daughter, Krista. They are only dangerous if they are treated meanly and abused. Our pit bulls are treated with lots of love and affection and are wonderful dogs. My veterinarian says pit bulls are one of the best breeds to have with children if the dog is brought up right. Pit bulls have a bad reputation because ignorant people train them to fight and attack. Tasha loves both my granddaughters, eighteen months and nineteen months old. She loves all the children and adults she meets.

**COULTER, GWENDOLEN RAE**
Watching my children discover the joys of life that I have begun to take for granted has brought new meaning into my life. This picture was taken at one of those moments: the moment my four-teen-month-old son got to play in the snow for the first time.

**COUNTRYMAN, EMILY**
I am a sixteen-year-old art student at Dreyfoos School of the Arts in West Palm Beach, FL. This

picture is of one of my Italian greyhounds, Princess. I originally took the picture so my mom could send it to her friends on an Italian greyhound mailing list, but when it was developed, I saw how cute she looked with her eyes squinting from the sun and just had to enter it.

## COUSINS, CAMILLE JADE
After a two-hour snorkeling expedition, my family and I relaxed on the sun-soaked beach of Kapas Island. While lounging in the shade of a small beach hut, I was in awe of the beautiful scenery: the blue-green of the sea and the golden sands. I was totally surrounded by the tropical colors of Malaysia's beauty, a beauty which had to be captured on film.

## COX, MATTHEW SOREN
I took this picture at nine o'clock in the morning after having only four hours of sleep. As I sat in that room trying to wake myself up, something about those five women affected me. I took the picture within seconds of glancing at them with the motivation of upsetting them because they, too, had just woken up. This picture represents me doing what I do best . . . being a joker.

## CROWE, JEAN ANN
Photography is a wonderful creative outlet for me. I can't imagine life without my camera. I was raised on a farm from 1960 until 1977. During this time, there were farms dotted across the prairie as far as you could see. Now, in my travels across the Midwest, I can see these abandoned farms from the highway. Sometimes I am overwhelmed with feelings of loss because these beautiful and proud places once provided for generations of families. It is a time that is gone, but will always be part of who I am.

## CULLEN, PATRICIA JEAN
I planted this tree approximately five years ago; it is a result of several clippings that have grown together. The sheer beauty of the tree needed to be captured on film.

## CUNNINGHAM, JOYCE RAE
This is my special friend, Lynx. He is a full-blooded Bengal cat who has a very outstanding personality. He loves to be where I am and included in whatever I am doing. The computer is one of our favorite things to do together; we spend endless hours exploring the internet.

## CUPIT, VICKI
I am the proud grandmommy of Michael, the world's first Viagra baby. Dr. Geofrey Sher pioneered the use of Viagra to build the lining of the uterus in infertile women. My daughter, Rene' Danford, used Viagra and thus became pregnant with Michael. Michael is expecting a Viagra sister in July, 2001. I photograph Michael a lot. I am a huge Chicago Bulls fan (and Michael fan) and this is by far one of the cutest photos I have ever taken!

## DAGLIO, YOLANDA A.
My Fujica is part and parcel of my travel gear; she interprets onto film what I see through my own eye. Trekking through Peru from big-city Lima to Inca on misty mountaintops, to condor flights over desert art in a plane without a door (for better shots of the Nazca lines), to viewing ancient cemeteries of decomposing mummies, to threading narrow cobblestone streets in the village of Pisac in the Sacred Valley of the Incas, I found two little sisters in the bustle of market day. I had ten seconds to focus, check the light, and press the shutter.

## DAIL, DIANA
This is our granddaughter, Tori. She had spent the night with us and was looking especially photogenic the next morning.

## DALEY, DAVID ARTHER
This is one of my five children at a fundraiser for the Girl Scouts at Ogemaw High School in northern Michigan. I copied the photo from video with no retouching. My wife and I do video recordings for events, and we are called The Time Machine.

## DANGERFIELD, JOSEPH
I have always been an animal-lover, and I have always enjoyed photography. However, I never really cared for small "yappy" dogs; that is until I met these two. Mattie and Chandler contain more combined personality than any other animal I know. They always do everything together, including taking naps. While I was sneaking up to take their photo, their eyelids and ears popped up in unison. I knew that was the moment to snap the shot.

## DASILVA, LESLIE ANNE
My name is Kei Kei, and I live in Moriches, Long Island. I am seven months old in this picture. My mom, Leslie, has taught me how to use the computer. If you look closely, you'll notice that there's a pet contest going on, and I am going to enter. Wish me luck!

## DAVIS, MERRILL BEDFORD
Photography allows one to capture an image of life and to portray genuine feelings, emotions, and colors so that we can remember or contemplate a moment in our lives. Seiko is a miniature pinscher who has become our best friend, true guardian, and here shows her true feelings as she looks adoringly at her human pal, Olympus.

## DEAL, MICHELE LYNN
When my daughter, Lesleyanne, was a toddler, I had to put away my drawing and painting gear because she kept getting into it. My sister-in-law placed a 35mm camera in my hands, and I fell in love and started painting with light. Lesleyanne is now nineteen years old, and photography is still my favorite form of expression. I was blessed to be able to capture this moment in time and it now hangs on the wall to be shared with everyone.

## DEERING, TIM J.
This photo was taken while on a camping trip with my family. My wife, Charlotte, and I were sitting in our campsite watching the sunset when I took this photo.

## DEMAREST, STEPHEN LYLE
This picture was taken while I was on a trip to England last summer with the Boy Scouts of the United States. I feel this is one of my best photos out of the fifteen rolls of film I took on this three-week trip.

## DEMIERO, VICKI
Meet Luige, my best buddy. At a year old, Luige still had the innocence and uncertainty of a puppy. We'd had a foot of snow that morning. I looked out the window to see how Luige was taking this white stuff. Snow, what's that? Luige was laying down, totally covered with snow. I could see his ears and tail. As I approached, he stood up and shook off some of the snow. He looked up at me as I snapped this picture. I totally understood the expression on his face. What do you think?

## DESCHÊNES, DOMINIQUE
This is a picture of my daughter, Laurie. She was only eighteen months old at this time and began to make discoveries. It's a period in a child's life when they really deserve to be photographed and engraved in our memories. Children have a capacity for making us rediscover the miracles that surround us. This flower is only an example between the others.

## DESORDA, MICHAEL ELY
Michael DeSorda's passion is displaying to the world the wondrous and fascinating land sculpture of our planet, not necessarily portrayed in its natural shape, form, and color, but rather Michael's interpretation of landscapes. Leaving behind constraints, Michael has crossed that chasm where photography moves from a technical endeavor to an artistic achievement. Michael, though a native southern Californian in both body and mind, currently lives in Hastings, MN, with his wife and two teenage daughters.

## DILLE, DAWN LOUISE
These are two of my triplets, the biggest, Faith Anne, and the smallest, Hannah Nicole. They were born August 19, 1999, and they are the apples of my eye. My only regret is that their other sister isn't in the picture.

## DRAY, BECKY
This is a photo of my daughter, Lexy. She wasn't quite sitting up on her own yet, so when I propped her up in the arm of the couch, she lit up! She was all dressed up for a birthday party and was definitely the hit of the party!

## DU'JARDIN, ROO
I have always been fascinated by the minutiae of nature, having photographed with macro equipment now for twenty-five years. Being able to capture detail the naked eye cannot reveal is a visually rewarding experience for me. "Mycena" was photographed using bellows and a macro lens; it was the tallest mushroom standing only five millimeters high. I returned the following day to re-shoot these curious tiny mushrooms embedded in moss on a tree branch, only to find they had expired. Time, along with magnitude, exists on a different scale in this diminutive world.

## DUARTE, JULIE
This is my daughter, Shelby, five, and my stepson, Danny, twelve. It's hard on kids with siblings growing up in separate households. This is the case with Danny and Shelby. Although they only

get to see each other every other weekend, most of their time is spent swimming, playing, and, as you can see, teaching Shelby how to ride her bike. What time they do have together is time well spent. Danny and Shelby share a special bond, and, as you can see, a picture is worth a thousand words.

**DULAK, HENRY**
Spring of 2001 must have been perfect for this echinopsis cactus to produce such a floral arrangement. It's easy to miss seeing its display of beauty because the blossoms only last a day. By late afternoon they are gone! I moved from Mosinee, WI, to Valle del Oro a few years ago and really enjoy photographing all the desert has to offer. A couple of my other photographs have been published in the local newspaper. I do all my photography with an Olympus D500L digital camera. While I long for the latest and greatest, this camera serves me well!

**DUNHAM, SARAH B.**
As my Aunt Nancy and I drove towards California from Arizona, I noticed a beautiful stretch of mountain. I couldn't help but stare in awe at its incredible wonder and timelessness as I took the best snapshots of the whole trip. This picture will always be a reminder of how beautiful this earth truly is.

**DYCHE, MATT**
This is a rare photo of a white-tailed deer taken from my parents' property in Idaho. The deer was born on that land and is still thriving today. I am very new to the photography world and am very proud of this picture. I guard this deer from year to year, ensuring its survival.

**EDFORS, RONALD D.**
I've lived with this powerful river all my life. To capture in pictures man's desire to harness the strength and depth of the waters always amazes me.

**EDWARDS, MARTY C.**
It would be almost impossible to explain this picture. It would take knowing Martin to fully understand this capture of uniqueness. Let your imagination go wild as you laugh at his expression and form your own conclusion as to the rhyme of reason.

**EISEN, NICOLE**
Trekking along a Blue Mountain trail, west of Sydney, Australia, a ray of light shone onto my head and I went "snap."

**ELLSWICK, CHRYSTIE ANN K. LEE**
Pictures say a lot more than words. Every moment is important, and capturing those moments are important to me. I have three beautiful children and, believe me, the film and pictures are endless. I love taking pictures of every little thing they do so I can share them with my grandchildren one day. This is a picture of my daughter, Cassandra, when she was two years old. I was amazed at how natural she seemed as she talked with her granny while cooking breakfast for the family. She'll be a wonderful mama one day, but she'll always be my "Lil' Mama."

**ELPERS, RHONDA K.**
"Rain Day" is one of many hundreds of photos I've taken of my pets. On this particular day, it was raining outside, and the cats all seemed interested in watching and listening to the rain. If I ever choose a second career, it will be in nature and pet photography. I am currently a project manager for a software company. I live with my husband and children, three cats, and one dog outside Atlanta, GA.

**ENCISO, JOMAR J.**
It was a lazy afternoon in San Francisco, and I was just sitting around trying to find a subject to shoot. But I could not find any! So I looked and saw the reflections of the buildings and decided to just shoot it. Then I went home. I always tell my fiancée, Priscilla, that I only needed "one" shot to prove to myself that I could do this.

**ESPINOSA, JOHN**
A nameless figure wanders in a strange land. Confusion frozen on his face, the sun shines like uncertainty in his eyes. Exhausted and beaten, yet he goes on. The crowd behind him turns away, unaware of his strife. Although I did not truly know him, his emotion is something to which we can all relate. This is dedicated to my mother, Jenny, and grandmother, Andromahi, for raising me with love; to my brother, Demetri, for growing up with me; and finally, to Jim, for being like a father and for having faith in me.

**EVERHART, LEONA L.**
When I took this picture, I was totally shocked at how it turned out. My husband and I live and breath our business and don't get a whole lot of free time to enjoy the beautiful things around us. So we have this picture on both of our desktops at work to give us a quick fix of one of God's beautiful creations, next to our four beautiful children that is: Christopher, twenty-one, Crystal, fourteen, Cayla, thirteen, and Ricky Jr., eleven. To my husband, with your love and presence in my life, I know the true meaning of "Serenity." I love you, Rick.

**FALKOWSKI, VINCENT**
Phalaenopsis is commonly known as the moth orchid. I have pursued the perfect orchid and subsequently the perfect picture. I may never fully succeed in that perfection; however, I feel that this picture captures the truly delicate nature and elegance of the flower. Most of my photographs have been captured on film. "Simply White" is my first published digital photo.

**FALTO, EVELYN**
I love taking pictures. One day while our daughters were playing in the backyard, my somewhat crazy husband, John, put Mitnite, our Labrador puppy, on my daughter's bike. For a moment it looked like Mitnite was ready to take off. Well, Mitnite is now two years old and insists we take the training wheels off.

**FARNSWORTH, THURLOW CHARLES**
For me, catching this comet-of-the-century, partially framed by the circle of tree limbs, was the shot of the century.

**FEGEL, DANIEL L.**
My job requires that I use a camera to document accidents and health and safety violations. On occasion, everything is going right and instead of photographing violations I have the freedom to photograph a job well done. This is one of those instances. The guys in this picture have all requested a copy of it. There is a sense of pride in doing a good job, but there is an increase in self-worth when you can reflect back on the picture that captures that.

**FERNANDO, SANDRA ANN**
This is our unconventional guard dog, Jessie. She thinks she is a driver, and probably was in another life as she always looks for the opportunity to jump into the driver's seat. She is happiest there, as you can see from her big smile. We have tried convincing her that the Ontario driving department doesn't issue licences to those of the four-legged variety, but she pays us no heed. This works out fine, as when the vehicle is unattended, we don't require an alarm because who would dare steal it with a German shepherd grinning at the wheel?

**FILOV, ELLY**
I am always fascinated by this unique sculpture when I pass by it. I find it very intriguing since it lets the viewer make up their own story behind it. As an artist, I am drawn to the color contrast in this image: the bike's bright red metal frame juxtaposed over the white rock and green bushes. It's almost as if the bike is melting in with its background, yet it remains completely separate. I've recently started experimenting with photography and love the way I can capture the world around me on film.

**FISHER, ROBBIE**
My favorite vacation destination is France. I try to go there every few years and visit different regions each time I go. Sunflower fields are a common sight in the countryside. I found this field in full bloom near the town of Cognac.

**FLUEHR, GLENN KUHLMAN**
The last time I was in Waikiki, I was seven years old. Now living in Hawaii, I hardly recognize Waikiki. It's been over twenty years since I visited there. I felt this picture captured the warm feeling of the water and the beautiful scenery of Waikiki. My fiancée, Myrna, and I were walking along the beach, and we wanted to see the sun going down. The whole day made us feel closer together; it was the feeling of love, comfort, and warmth I get every time I look at this picture.

**FOELL, WANDA B.**
Sometimes when looking through my lens, the subject is narrowed down to a single focal point where what I see is intensified. To me, this photo spoke volumes. As I stood there looking at that pair of feet, I couldn't help but wonder where they had been and where they would end up. I saw the potential this moment had to show the reality of what homeless people face, so I took the shot. Now, thankfully, that opportunity exists.

**FOGELBERG, CARINA ANN**
My name is Carina. I am a sixteen-year-old girl in

tenth grade. I always take pictures of everything because the best moments are always unpredicted. In the picture, the mama cat is teaching her babies how to catch birds the easy way. I never thought about entering my photo into a contest, but when I heard of this one, I thought it would be fun. It is such a cute picture that I wanted others to see it, too. I am glad to have had this opportunity to share my photo, and I hope you like it.

### FONTENOT, MICHELLE BRIGETTE
I love taking photos of animals and nature. This photo is of my friend, Danny's, dog, Shakita. I was at the right place at the right time. She was lounging on his bed, and I started snapping just as she happened to be yawning. My dream is to one day have enough money to open up an animal rescue shelter. I have four dogs and three cats, all of which have been adopted or rescued from the streets.

### FORDHAM, GRAEME TREVOR
Thank you for choosing "Last Summer" ur choice in the competition. I took this photo because it was the most stunning sunset throughout the entire summer. There were other sunsets, but this one appealed to me most. Photography is an extension of my personality and a good way of expressing yourself. We live in Manukau Harbour, looking towards the West Coast where the sun sets. Photography has always been a bit of a hobby for me for many years, and I am on the lookout for a good photo every time we go out. My camera is with me at all times. I work at a large printing firm from which I was able to further my education. My spare time is taken up with two daughters and seven grandchildren, so there are lots of opportunities to use my camera. Photos are a statement and are very hard to replace.

### FRANCO, MARIA ELENA
My love for photography always draws my attention to interesting events around me. One Sunday evening, I saw these boys trying hard to reach for something that was in the trash bin. I was glad they didn't take any notice of me because once they see you the spell is broken, so I was able to take a few pictures of them. I chose this title because this picture reminded me that some people's garbage is another person's treasure.

### FRANKEN, TODD
Skydiving is the ultimate freedom and a great photo opportunity. When tandem skydiving over Coolidge, AZ, from Mike Mullin's King Air Summer 2001, strap a camera to your head, and go! Promote safe skydiving at a dropzone near you or contact the United States Parachute Association for information about skydiving.

### FRAYER, KEMBERLEY
My fiancé and I were on vacation, and when I was standing outside the door of our hotel, this beautiful view left me in a state of awe. I just had to try and capture it with my camera. To my surprise, I got it, and it turned out wonderful. I hope others enjoy this wonderful view as we have.

### FUCHS, MIKE THOMAS
"Red Devils" is a picture of the loves of my life and myself as we show that a little bit of snow is not going to keep us down! With about seven feet of snow on the ground, I still took both machines for rides all winter long.

### GASTON, SANDRA K.
My three-day-old grandson, Zachary, is being held by his seven-year-old brother, Seth. Their proud parents are Robert and Shawne Martin. They live in Bon Secour, AL, and I live in Silverhill, AL, which is in southwest Alabama. Seth declared that he heard Zachary call him Bubba when he was less than twenty-four hours old.

### GAYRE, JOI
Our four-month-old son, Payton Thomas, was the most precious gift under the tree on Christmas 2000. He is such a delight and so photogenic. This picture was a big hit with the rest of our family. At the time this picture was taken, we were living in Crete, Greece. Payton is a world traveler even at such a young age.

### GENOVESE, JAMIE L.
My husband and I moved into this hobby farm about a month before I took this picture. The girls were part of the package, friendly, inquisitive, and helpful in the gardens, barn, and, yes, even the house. My niece, A. J., and nephew, Ryan, couldn't wait to come from the city to see Auntie Jamie's chickens. It was truly an unforgettable moment!

### GERMAIN, CAROL M.
I love taking my beautiful granddaughter, Claudia Angelique Germain, to the park when she honors me with a visit. Despite all the play equipment available to her at eighteen months of age, Claudia was already aware of the most rewarding kinds of interaction. Although she lived in Ontario when this photograph was taken, she recently moved to Kelowna, and we are anticipating many more happy moments together here in Summerland, BC, Canada.

### GIBSON, CYNTHIA D.
This full moon was captured as it took its time setting. I also took this opportunity to look at the Arizona sunrise. I am pleased that my first picture with a digital camera has been selected for this publication, as it is my mother's favorite photo. Taking photos is a hobby I have enjoyed for a long time. I visualize almost everything I see as a potential picture of beauty and interest. A photo captures one moment in time and holds on to that instant for others to enjoy for a lifetime. As a self-taught amateur photographer, moving to Arizona has given a renewed and refreshing inspiration to my hobby.

### GILBREATH, TARA LEE
This is a photo of my daughter and our pet rabbit, Bunz. This photo is very special to me because it was taken on her first Easter Sunday; it reminds me of the perfect day together. To photograph children is very important because it is so precious when you catch that perfect expression, which makes a memory for a lifetime.

### GILLINGS, ANNALIISA
I took the photo in Idaho on the way to my first wilderness training. I have been back to Idaho twice since, and several times to other parts of America. Before that, apart from traveling in Europe, I had only been to Florida to visit Disney World with my daughter when she was small. I've loved taking photos ever since I got my first Brownie box camera as a little girl in Finland, where I grew up. Some shots are better than others, and every now and then there is a jewel. Thanks for the opportunity.

### GISKEØDEGÅRD, MARGARETH
One morning a fairytale-like scene woke me up. This view gave birth to an inspiration to create a painting called "A Cherub Watches the Sunrise Over Mountains."

### GIVANS, CAROL LYNN
Trip is looking for our friendly backyard squirrel. He is a year old in this picture. He belongs to my daughter, Chrissy, and her husband, Eddie.

### GNANAPRAKASHAM, CYRIL
It was my first outing with my friends, Jaiku and Rehka, after I landed in the United States on November 4, 2000. We were on our way back from Point Loma in San Diego, CA, on a gloomy afternoon during Thanksgiving weekend. When this place caught my attention, I was tempted to take a picture of it, not knowing that it would find a place for itself in *Sketches of the Eye*.

### GOMES, MAUREEN
Jaromir was presented with the Art Rose Trophy in June 2001 for the fourth consecutive year. This National Hockey League award is given to the player who has scored the most points overall in a season. He has won two Stanley Cups and has been a Pittsburgh Penguin for all of his eleven years in the league. When I took this photograph, I had no idea that he would no longer be a player on my team after the 2000–2001 season. Due to his impending trade, I may never have the privilege of photographing him in uniform again. Goodbye, Jaromir. Our hearts will be with you wherever you go.

### GOWER, FRANCES JOYCE
My darling granddaughter, Che, was born in Australia just one week before the passing of her great-grandmother in England. Knowing neither would ever meet in person and hence the chance of a treasured photograph impossible, I placed an image of Che in the arms of her great-grandmother, Vaughan, who is pictured here with her husband, Gordon. This photograph brings together two treasures, my mum, Vaughan, and Che. This is something that Che and our family will cherish forever.

### GREGOIRE, PATSY M.
My husband's name is Clyde, and we have one son named Kelly. We own and operate a small family business in Dominion City. We live on approximately twenty-three acres on the outskirts of town along the Roseau River. I enjoy doing crafts and taking pictures of which many are taken on our scenic property. While cutting grass in our backyard, I spotted the butterflies and sat for three-quarters of an hour to catch "Beauty" sitting just right. My friend, Rita Mazurski, always

enjoyed my pictures and entered this photo for me.

**GUIDER, WENDY JOY**
No one ever thought they would make it. The past two years were filled with trials and tribulations for their relationship. When no one was there to support them, they held on to each other and their love grew stronger. Everyone said they would never make it, but their young hearts knew differently. While everyone else planned their relationships' end, they planned out their perfect day. It was "The Perfect Day" where true love proved it could make it through anyone or anything that stood in its way.

**GUNNLAUGSSON, EINAR**
This photo of the Snæfells Glacier is a view a beautiful place named Arnarstapi where many people come every summer to feel the energy that is said to come from the glacier. The glacier is considered to be one of the seven major energy centers on Earth. The snowless mountain Stapafell is at the southern part of the glacier. Iceland is a paradise for photographers not only for its beautiful landscape, towns, and villages, but for the colors and the light, as well, which are unique in Iceland. In one of my walks by the sea south of the glacier, I could not resist taking this photo of the view in front of me. And I must say that it turned out to my satisfaction.

**GURSKY, MELONI**
This picture should have been titled "Impatient!" This is what can happen when your friends take too long to get ready to go snorkeling (Florida Keys 1999).

**HALE, RICK E.**
When I took this picture, I had just started in photography. I was walking in a forest preserve past this pond and really liked the way the clouds reflected off the water. I snapped the picture and moved on looking for something more interesting, maybe an animal or a dragonfly. This was the only decent picture on the roll, and it really impressed family and friends. This picture, I think, really shows the need to conserve the natural beauty around us.

**HAMMACK, DARREL R.**
After receiving a new camera as a gift from my son, I began taking all sorts of pictures. A young family friend, Nikki, after seeing some of my photographs, asked if I could take some photos of her. That day I took over eighty of Nikki. After viewing them, I was so surprised at how perfect this shot was of her. It seemed to completely capture her playfulness and charm. I have a large print of it in my home and at my office. Even now when I look at it, I am amazed at how well it turned out. I now take pictures all the time and am eager to see other photos turn out just as perfectly.

**HANCOCK, NICHOLAS SIMON**
I took this on vacation in 2000. My wife, Rebecca, and I decided to go on a proper road trip instead of a beach holiday, and we drove two thousand miles around the Pacific Northwest and Canada. We spent just a day in Glacier National Park, Montana, crossing to get to Calgary.

Nothing prepared us for how beautiful it was; coming from England, we have nothing as spectacular as this. We could have easily spent the whole trip there. I took lots of photos on that trip, but this one was actually snapped from our car window and brings back great memories.

**HARPER, WESLEY K.**
Since childhood, I've always loved trains, especially fast, sleek, passenger trains. Newark's small station is primarily for local rail service. It carries passengers to and from Philadelphia with many stops in between. Amtrak stops here twice a day. The train in the photo didn't at that time. Traveling at one hundred mph, the train was captured with just the right shutter speed. I loved taking this shot.

**HARRIS, BETTY**
After a hurricane, we had lost two trees. My husband, Bill Harris, cut them up and stacked them in the backyard. After admiring his hard work, we decided to paint smiley faces on them. That winter it snowed, and I took this picture. It always brings a smile to my face and memories of a good time.

**HEDIN, TINA MARIE**
I've enjoyed taking pictures of animals and nature for as long as I've been traveling. A trip to Africa was not only a personal dream come true but a nature photographer's fantasy. These sister lions and their cubs were the highlight of an extraordinary trip. The safari guide was even speechless at this sight!

**HEMMICK, KAY**
Matthew 3:11, He shall baptize you with the Holy Spirit and with fire. Our son, John Hemmick, was baptized in the Boerne Lake on October 3, 1999. As we approached the lake, a cloud billowed overhead. When our boy was dipped into the water, a cloud opened up and a gentle rain fell on our faces (come Holy Spirit and rain down). In the photo, the rain reminds us that we are baptized with water and the sunset reminds us we are baptized by the Holy Spirit with fire. The grace of our Lord Jesus Christ be with you all, Revelation 22:21.

**HENDRICKS, MICHAEL THOMAS**
It was a dark stormy night in Wyoming, with temperatures in the minus teens and a wind-chill factor of minus sixty-five degrees. Snow was blowing with near white-out conditions. Ice covered the road and made it nearly impossible to drive. It took eight hours to make the crossing of one hundred miles from Cheyenne to Laramie, having to stop numerous times to chip ice from the windshield. Upon making the treacherous trek safely, this was found on my tire. "Trucker's Flower" is dedicated to all truckers worldwide for the outstanding job they do.

**HERMOGENO, MICHAEL ANTHONY**
This is a photo I took of my godson with a Canon AE-1, which was handed down to me by my godfather. I love taking pictures of my nieces and nephews, and their poses have become more natural as the years go by. Featured in this picture is

Nicholas Abaunza, but you should see his sister, Ashley, and cousins, Kristen and Tyler Soriano!

**HICKS, AMY MICHELLE**
This is a photo of the family pet. He has been a part of my husband's life for a long time, and I now get the pleasure of sharing a love for this wonderful cat.

**HILL, ERIC**
This is a photo of my niece, Katie Martin Hewitt, with her puppy, Rosa Belle. The puppy had been napping when Katie started talking baby talk to her. It looks like Rosa Belle is trying to get Katie to be quiet. The picture was more or less a mistake. I was just taking random photos and this one just happened. Sometimes those are the best!

**HILLIKER, MARTHA ANN**
This picture was taken on a cold March day. The star was produced for placement as the entrance to the new Texas history museum. This picture was taken just as the thirty-five-foot star was being lifted off of the semi that brought it to the location. I caught it just as the two cranes were moving the star to get it in position. After the placement of the star on its pedestals, visitors could walk under the thirty-five-foot tall bronze star. I took this picture because of the angle and simplicity of the star. In reality it took hours of preparation to get the star to this point. The family that built the star slept with it the night before it was moved to make sure it was safe. I always take my camera to special events in hopes of getting that one special shot.

**HINDMON, WANDA FAYE**
Smokey was asleep on the couch when I reached for the camera. He woke up with a yawn just as I snapped the picture. He wasn't mad though; Smokey is a happy cat, and only one of six in my household.

**HOLLAND, RHONDA L.**
Meet Baby, a three-year-old domestic short-hair. When she first came to us, we noticed a problem and found out she had a bad heart valve. The vet said she wouldn't live over a year. Now, almost three years later, she's playing on the computer. Whenever I am on the computer, Baby is there, walking in front of the screen or sitting on the back of the chair watching me. Baby and her family live on a farm in South Dakota.

**HOLLAND, ROY A.**
After retiring from the electronic field, my love of photos became my hobby. I see a photograph as a window to the past. Nature with natural lighting is my favorite subject. Colors are brilliant. A good photo lives forever even though the event is long gone. This photo was taken about ninety miles north of Las Vegas, NV, at the Pahranagant Wildlife Reserve. The unique setting of nature shows the past history of the area. The high water marks on the dead trees show how much the water has dropped in the past years. The overall beauty of the area is fantastic.

**HOLM, JUDIE PATRICIA**
The name of the glacier is Salmon Glacier, located north of Hyder, AR. I was at a school reunion

in August in Terrace, BC, when I decided to motor four hours to Stewart, BC, and Hyder, AK. The most breathtaking scenery is on that route, as well as between Terrace, BC, and Prince Rupert, BC, Canada. I'm an actress, so when I'm not in front of the camera, I'm behind one snapping photos. My hobby has always been photography. It is my relaxation and my way to enjoy nature at its best! My first camera was a Brownie with a detachable flash, given to me on my twelfth birthday. When it comes to photography, my philosophy is that beauty is in the eye of the beholder!

## HOLMES, JOHN

Having lived on the East Coast and seeing the Atlantic Ocean many times, I was engulfed by the beauty of the Atlantic from the shores of West Africa so much so that I thought I would share its beauty with those who may not have the opportunity to see the Atlantic Ocean's other unspoiled side.

## HOPKINS, WILSON HODGE

This photo was taken near my home in Trinity. Although I took photography lessons from Seattle Filmworks, I do it only as a hobby. I enjoy taking pictures. I have a large collection of pictures of wild animals, pets, and icebergs.

## HOUFEK, VLADIMIR

This picture of Air France 747 was taken by me on our trip in St. Maarten. I just purchased a new MVC Sony FD 91 digital camera. My wife and I love to travel, and photography is my hobby. I also enjoy drawing.

## HOWE, TINA M.

This is a photo of my stepdaughter, Mercedes, and her new baby brother, Noah. Mercedes has been totally in love with Noah since the moment he was born. Noah was three weeks old in this picture, and Mercedes had drawn a face on her hand and was trying to make him smile. Before long, they had snuggled into the rocking chair and were fast asleep. This became a ritual with them that continued on nineteen months later. Mercedes says that when they cuddle, Noah steals her energy. I know just how she feels.

## HU, BAO Z.

I was impressed with the unique design of this building, Acros Fukuoka. It is designed environmentally friendly and energy efficient. This building, located in front of Tenjin Park in Fukuoka, Japan, is designed with stepped terraces towards the park. These terraces are so intensely planted that they form an insulation layer as well as a greened surface. You can enjoy these terraces accessed from the park. Unlike other surrounding buildings, this office is indeed a great extension of the park. The interior features an atrium throughout all floors. The operable opening on the top of the atrium and the windows facing the terraces form a natural ventilation system.

## HUGHES, CHRIS A.

I am a twenty-two-year-old amateur photographer from Toronto, Canada, with an extreme passion for photography. I love the challenge of trying to capture life's wonders on film. Hopefully my pictures will inspire others in the preservation of our environment. The sounds of early morning birds awakened me. The smell of a spring morning dew drew me. The atmosphere inspired me, and God's creations amazed me. It was then that I realized nature is always, yet never the same. Stop to appreciate life and all its surroundings. Enjoy the miracle called life.

## HUGHES, CRISTY JOE

Aubree was so intrigued by the bluebonnets that we couldn't even get her to look up at us; but it still made for a timeless beautiful picture. She was just learning to sit up, and I'm surprised she didn't fall over! Aubree was seven months old at this time. Mommy and Daddy love you so much and are so proud of you!

## HUNT, CHRISTINA STRATIS

I developed my interest in photography from my grandfather. As a young girl, I remember spending many days with my granddaddy in his photography shop. I loved having the ability to capture life in a picture. My six animals keep me busy finding that perfect moment to cherish. Sofie and Murphy made it happen for me in this picture.

## HUNT, GRACE

This picture was taken at Grandma and Grandpa's house in Tracy, CA. Sierra was only three months old, and Joshua was thirty-four months old. We've traveled back and forth from Hawaii three times so far since Sierra was born because their father is in the U.S. Navy, stationed in Pearl Harbor on a submarine. It's tough being a military family, but traveling overseas is great fun!

## HWA, NANCY WONG YAN

Maybe it's the color blue. Looking up at the sky, I admire the white fluffy clouds gliding across the blue unlimited sky. Well, that's what I love to do—no boundary, just pure freedom. In the same light, I love the sea as much as the sky, maybe even more. I believe I have in me the great spirit of the whales and dolphins. Pure freedom is what they told me.

## HYLAND, JOSEPHINE

It was a nice summer's day at the Melbourne Zoo in Australia, and I just couldn't resist taking a photo of the lion as he lay there watching the lionesses in the adjoining enclosure. The following day the lion cubs went on display.

## IYER, SHANKAR

The story of the ugly duckling who became a beautiful swan fascinated me in my childhood. The swans in the lake garden in the Royal Botanical Gardens in Toronto provided me with a perfect opportunity to go back to my childhood with my adorable son, Gune, and shoot the swans without killing them. It has also given me a great thrill that you have selected one of my photos for publication!

## JACKS, JERI LEE

Every evening, no matter what time of year, I have picture-perfect views of sunsets over my pond. No one view is ever the same. This particular evening, the water was still and the sight was breathtaking. I knew I had to get it on film. I keep my camera ready at all times and I have an album full of beautiful views. I have my own cleaning business and I am a Mary Kay consultant.

## JANUARY, CHRISTINA MICHELLE

I feel it is important to capture every moment on film and to preserve its significance for a lifetime. This black-and-white photo of my daughter, Haleigh, was one of the first black-and-white photos I have taken. I chose a park in Oklahoma, where we are from, to achieve this image because of its resplendent magnificence. From my experience, I can say that the best photo you can acquire is the one most natural. My daughter has given me an excellent opportunity to explore my photographic vision.

## JOHNSTON, DIANE

My mischievous kittens provide me with many photo opportunities. When I saw Annie crawl out of the dishwasher, I grabbed my digital camera. I have always used my 35mm for my family pictures and creative photos, but as a realtor, I use my digital for business because of its convenience. This photo proves that you can be creative with any camera, especially when you have an interesting subject like my Annie.

## JOLLY, DEBORAH WRAY

Tucked away on the bank of the Rio Grande is a little unknown hot spring. During a road trip through New Mexico, I decided to take my friends to this natural hot tub. It is quite a hike from the road, but the view of the river valley is breathtaking. Before we reached the spring, this photo was taken after our exhausting hike to the riverbank.

## JUTRAS, ROBERT GENE

When I took this photo, I thought about how tranquil life can be when one stops and looks around. Different surroundings can bring tranquility to different people. When life gets too busy, this is my tranquility, along with my family, Alisha, Kyle, and Miranda.

## KAHL, GEORGE WILLIAM

This was the first picture taken on our first day in Napa, CA, at the first winery. I took this picture as I watched this bud open for the first time.

## KARUMBAIAH, VIKRAM

I've dreamt of traveling to the United States for a long time. I've often wondered what it would be like in a place where bluegrass and hard rock co-exist! This picture, to me, signifies the beginning of an exciting and beautiful journey here in the United States. Vive la "Liberty!"

## KAUMEYER, ALVIN G.

Photography allows an opportunity for uniqueness. I try to share my visual experiences with others.

## KELLER, DIXON WILLIAM

This photo was taken by my wife, Christine, an excellent amateur portrait photographer, with a Canon EOS Rebel 2000. It was digitally remastered by me, having removed a bridge and people in the background. This is a picture of me giving a congratulatory hug to my son, Jameson, who was just promoted to cadet chief E-7 in the U.S.

Naval Cadets. He is the first cadet chief petty officer in the nation, hence the title "Pride." The photo was taken on the Willamette River in Portland next to the USS Blue SS-581.

**KELLY, MATTHEW EMERSON**
Photography is my favorite hobby, but seldom do shots like this one turn out better than expected. This June sunset in Minnesota perfectly captured this peaceful moment. The photo makes it hard to believe, but I am actually lying on the dock, leaning out over the water! I was so concerned I'd fall in with my camera. I'd forgotten the photo completely until the film came back from the developer! My good friend, Andy, has a large copy of this image hanging in his home.

**KERBY, GLEN**
This photo of our son, James Nehemiah Kerby, was taken when he was about three months old. I'm delighted to have captured his sweet disposition and easy smile. He is the light of our eyes, and our prayer for him is that he will grow to be mighty in spirit and a light to his generation. My interest in photography comes via my mother, Mrs. Doreen Kerby of Saskatoon, Saskatchewan, Canada. Herself a talented and accomplished travel photographer, Mum brings vivacity and heart to each picture she takes. How wonderful that James and Grandma Doreen have a very special relationship.

**KERN, MEGAN LYNN**
This is a photograph I took this spring in my studio at school. I enjoy music and playing it, and recently I started photographing musical instruments. I also like to photograph reflections of things. I combined the two and out came "Musical Reflection" for all to enjoy.

**KIMREY, LUCINDA ANN**
This is a picture of my husband, Mark, kissing our daughter, Genevieve. It is definitely one of my favorites.

**KLASSEN, LENA**
I've always enjoyed taking pictures, and in all my fifty or more years in doing this, have never entered one in a contest. This is a real surprise and special treat for me. In the photo, left to right, are Rascal (Cairn female), Christopher, and Bear (males of the same litter). These animals had a habit of looking out the door when spring was around the corner. This time I caught all three doing so at the same time. Rascal was a few years older than the cats and loved to play "chase and run" with her humans, taking turns chasing and running. The cats couldn't seem to catch on to the game. When one would turn and face her, she thought the game was on and would start running around the house waiting to be caught, only to turn around and find the cat gone. You could almost see the disappointment in Rascal's face when she realized the cat wasn't chasing her.

**KNEREM, RON**
Back in '97, I was on my way to a music fest called Cornerstone. With all my friends surrounding me, the beauty of this picture will always remind me I was surely not alone. The

beauty in the sunlight of this picture is a wonder of God's own creation.

**KOLAR, ROBERT B., JR.**
This photo was taken during our honeymoon on Cayman Brac in the Cayman Islands. It was taken from inside a cave called "Rebecca's Cave." It's named this because in 1932 during a hurricane, families took shelter in it. A baby girl named Rebecca died during that storm. I had no idea that this photo was going to stand out from the rest of the great pictures we took. The lighting and the colors were perfect. I couldn't resist.

**KORN, RODNEY**
I like to search for beauty in the small things in life. This macro is a pair of small mushrooms. They seemed to have a personality of their own. In addition to photography, I enjoy motorcycling and piloting helicopters. I also love spending time with my three children, Tallon, Electra, and Xandria, and my wife, Elizabeth.

**KOZY, LAWRENCE S.**
For many, the rising sun heralds the beginning of a new day. For others, as the fishermen on the calm waters of Lake Malawi in South Central Africa, it's the setting sun that acts as an alarm clock. Watching the fishermen in their dugout canoes load their nets and paddle to the prime spots for a healthy catch while the sun's fire is extinguished in the water is a favorite memory of my visit. The serenity of this photo is a true reflection of the simplicity and beauty of the people from the warm heart of Africa—Malawi.

**KRAMER, ROBERT, JR.**
During my battle with A.L.S. (Lou Gehrigs Disease), I have lost so much. But I refuse to allow it to take my ability to share a little piece of Heaven with everyone who cares to join me. Have a beautiful day.

**KRAVTSOV, KONSTANTINE VASILEVICH**
This is a really good book!

**KRAUS, ALAN BRIAN**
When traveling alone on my first trip to California, exhausted, I was looking for a roadside rest stop. Instead, I encountered the stunning grounds that led me to the San Simeon estate. I've always maintained confidence in my artist's eye, with no training or participation in classes at all. In sum, I prefer to focus on the beauty of our world. The charming antiquity of San Simeon did the trick.

**KRENKE, CINDY**
We moved into this wonderful old farmhouse two-and-a-half years ago. I've enjoyed taking pictures of all of our chickens, geese, ducks, sunsets—lots of summer shots—but this sunny, winter day was irresistible! Each day the sun shone on the side of the house, causing the icicles to melt. At night, with the cold weather, the stalactites would freeze solid, growing longer and longer each day. The shadow on the house is from the huge old oak tree in our yard. My husband, Chris, two sons, Derrick and Cody, and I enjoy our simple life on the farm.

**KRITNER, SANDRA ANN**
This is one of my favorite photos of my daughter, Amanda Kritner. She is holding her newborn cousin, Paige Padgett, born minutes earlier on April 6, 2001.

**KROON, JOEL D.**
This was just one of many beautiful sunsets that happen in central Florida. While going out to eat one night, I turned around in the parking lot and saw this beautiful sight. A picture is worth a thousand words.

**LaFORTE, ANITA**
This is a photograph of our home in springtime located in the New York Mid-Hudson Valley. Buying this Queen Anne Victorian was the fulfillment of a dream of mine since I was seven years old. We were lucky that it has been kept in impeccable original condition, considering the house is 130 years old. The interior is full of meticulously restored original antique ornamentations. It's situated on a lovely three-acre park-like piece of property that includes a carriage house. We love the changes of the four seasons; however, it's especially nice during springtime when the flower gardens are in full blossom.

**LAHEY, NATASHA FAY**
This is a photo of my daughter, Madelyn. I really enjoy taking photos, especially of my daughter. She seems to be very photogenic and is a very good subject. I took this photo to put into her Christmas photo frame.

**LAKE, ANNETTE**
Having fun in west Yellowstone is a family tradition. We have been enjoying the snow, wildlife, and hospitality for six years. It is a shame the park will close for snowmobiling; many will miss the beauty.

**LANE, MICHAEL**
Photographs can not only capture a spectacular image or a fond memory, but like all art, they can create or enhance emotion and thought. I try to take photos that have similar qualities. Whilst this photo carries a great deal of sentimental value for me, I can only hope that it can be appreciated in some way by all those who see it.

**LARSSON, BERITH M. I.**
I was riding my bike when I saw this relaxed but colorful young man. He reminded me of a palette—black skin, red hair, blue beer, green grass, and yellow flowers in the sunset. It was just outstanding!

**LASAM, LOIDA C.**
This picture shows the simple beauty that I see in my friends and family, and the innocence and simple fun that we have together when we take and pose for pictures. This is the essence of the pictures that I take: just pose whichever way you're comfortable; just pose any which way you like; just pose; smile and there will be beauty caught in a picture naturally . . . just like in this one.

**LAUER, LINDA M.**
We had just moved into our new home when I saw this photo opportunity. Pictured here is my tor-

toise shell calico cat. Zena is a year old here with my son, James', kitten, Zoe. Six months earlier, Zena was hit by a car. My son, John, held her during the ride to the animal hospital. It is a miracle that she survived. Zoe was rescued by James when she was about six weeks old. They are very happy now and never leave the yard. I love taking pictures, but this is the first time I ever entered a photo contest.

## LAWS, SHAUN
In the dull light of this chilly morning, I perched my camera precariously on the wall fronting Jagannath Temple. The slowly-lifting fog tinged Durban Square with a gray cast that dampened its usual vibrancy. An occasional puja (offering) of corn kept my feathered subjects in place as I waited for a human element to enter the frame. With the birds continuously roused from their feeding, I restrained my twitching finger from pressing the shutter release until I had the desired composition. My patience was rewarded when this man entered the scene and the pigeons scattered before him in a fractured veil of feathers.

## LEICH, BRETT
This is my niece, Angela, eleven months old, playing in the leaves at Grandma and Grandpa's house last fall. She was having so much fun and was infatuated with the feel of the leaves. I decided to take the camera out and just started snapping shots. She loves having her picture taken, and this picture turned out especially nice because she decided to pick up the leaf and hold it for me.

## LEMIEUX, AMANDA LATHA
This is a photo of my baby, a macaw named Romeo. He was sitting in his favorite tree, eating a treat that I had set there for him. I was getting ready to take a photo of him eating the treat, but as soon as he saw the camera he posed. He stood up straight, held his head up, and held still until I had taken the picture. That wasn't what I had originally planned, but he had his own ideas. I was pleasantly surprised when I saw the photo; it came out pretty well. I guess he knows what he's doing!

## LIGHTSEY, ROBERT LAUREN
This is a picture of my friend, Oscar, taken at break time.

## LIJFFIJT, TANJA
This van was my transportation and place to sleep on my trip for healing and self-discovery. I discovered how powerful the brain is and how my way of thinking controls my life! I learned how to train my brain and to live peacefully and in harmony without unnecessary fears or past thoughts. I became my own best friend and I am truly happy now. I wrote a book on this trip with some simple exercises and pictures. I hope that many people become truly happy and see their lives in a different perspective. Much love, The Little Dutch Girl.

## LINKMEYER, LISA
This picture was taken in Kruger National Park in South Africa, one of my favorite game parks. The "Leopard" was pouncing around after a mouse or something really small, until he settled in this per-

fect spot ready to attack. It would have been a shot of a lifetime if he were going for larger prey. I am currently living in the United Kingdom and look forward to going home every year to try and capture some more amazing wildlife shots.

## LORD, DAMIAN MURRAY
This is a photo of our family dog, Jess, who has since passed away and is sadly missed. She was a very special loyal dog who really enjoyed going on outings with the family to the river, etc. I took this photo just two months prior to her death and was surprised it was picked but really pleased just the same. Now she will live on forever in this book.

## MacLEAN, LINDA MARY
This picture was taken on a family trip on a Boston Harbor Cruise. Britt is one of my eight beautiful grandchildren. I just took it because of the way the wind was blowing her beautiful hair and her big smile. She is just a gorgeous little girl, and this photo has captured her happiness and beauty forever.

## MADGE, DONNA MAY
I captured this photo, thanks to my husband, Steve. He called me outside on a chilly March night to look at the red northern lights. They are quite rare, so my first thought was to grab the camera and tripod. I shot a whole roll of film and captured a lot of good images, but this is my favorite. I love the challenge of timed exposures and am always amazed at the images I capture after dark.

## MAES, MARGARET A.
Taking snapshots has been a hobby in my family for three generations. I began with my mom's box camera. Taking photos of my family, my children, and my grandchildren is a tradition. The photo "Safe At Home" is of my granddaughter playing community softball. Through the years, I have entered a few contests and have won a few. A photo, to me, stops the clock. For that split second, that moment in time is forever frozen and preserved to be enjoyed again and again by generations to come.

## MAFFITT, DONALD M.
This is a photo of Mindy, my neighbor's Pomeranian. We were walking in the woods, along with my dog, Queen. There were a few inches of snow, and Mindy got it all over her face. I didn't realize how cute she was until I printed the picture later.

## MAINWARING-BERRY, JULIA
I'm an Australian visual artist, musician, and writer, who, by good fortune of birth and parentage, was brought up in an often zany and creative home. The main influence over my lifetime has been my late father, Geoffrey Mainwaring, an Australian second world war artist who has shared his love of people, art, and nature with all who expressed his same passion for art. To my parents, I am eternally grateful. Life is the most miraculous, creative experience. The artist attempts to illuminate the intangible essence of emotion, thought, feeling, and spirit. The poetry of life itself is to share an intimate moment in time,

which words cannot always adequately describe. The camera is my seeing eye, an exposure of myself, of my world, of the crowning jewels that make up the kaleidoscope of my life; this creation, this nature, they are a part of me as I am to them. In all of her magnificent moods, nature truly is an awesome spectacle! I thank God for the experience of being!

## MANAHAN, CHARLES
My photo was taken at Jim Andrew's seventieth birthday. The picture itself is self-explanatory. It was a surprise party given by his wife, Toots, and his daughter, my wife, Patty. The real surprise came when he found out his son, Jay, his wife, Bonni, and their families had come down from New Jersey to help him celebrate. Jim is a great man, loved by all who come in contact with him, but he has a special bond and love with my daughter, Meghan.

## MANGUM, BRANDY ELIZABETH
While serving in the United States Peace Corps in the beautiful country of Namibia, Africa, I had the pleasure of meeting some of the Himba people. Of the different cultures in Namibia, the Himba are the least westernized. This sand and thatch hut, set against the vast Opuwo horizon, houses ground henna that, when mixed with animal fat, is used to adorn the skin of Himba women.

## MANI, MOHAN KUMAR
During architecture school, I shot buildings, seeing life in inanimate structures. The gypsy in me found incredible solace in the companionship of my camera during my travels. People took easily to a grubby looking guy with a lost look and a camera. That's how I started photographing people. In San Diego, to meet architect James Hubbell, I was basking in the Hubbell's hospitality when I saw the three ladies of the family by the water. The backdrop and the light from the receding Californian sun only accentuated their humanity. It was all I could do to race to my camera.

## MANKE, GENEVA LEE
This is a picture of my grandson, Jacob, that I took the first time we met when he was five months old. I fell head over heels in love with him. The photo you see is a true black-and-white print that I developed at home and enhanced with oils and pencils. I enjoy the art of photography and hand-coloring.

## MANLEY, ROXANN LYVONNE
This is my daughter, Anastaja. While doing a school project at home, I had to place her in her crib so she wouldn't be underfoot. As you can tell by her expression, she didn't like it.

## MARFELL, GLENN FREDERICK
Some things in life do seem to be a little out of place. When hiking, most often you think of birds, wildlife, streams, and beautiful blue skies. However, once in a while something comes across one's mind that is a little out of the ordinary. Since beginning digital photography, I am rarely without my camera, and this time it paid off. The fireplug is one of my true finds while hiking; it's nice to feel safe from fire when out in the wilder

ness. I work with computer systems and love to take photographs whenever possible.

**MARSHALL, JENNIFER ROBIN**
I first want to thank the Lord above for creating such beauty as this to be photographed. The luna moth is one of the most beautiful in the world. My photo represents change as in life itself all around us. My love for nature stems back from my earliest memory as a child, where it was instilled in me by my parents, William and Hazel McCollum. I would also like to thank my friend, Melonie Byrd, for believing in my talent. Thanks to everyone involved in publishing my photo. It is dedicated to my three-and-a-half-year-old grandson, Chase Larussa.

**MARTIN, CAMILLE**
We were leaving for my parents' home on Easter Sunday, and I saw this beautiful field of wildflowers at the entrance to their subdivision. My daughter, Taylor, wanted to stop and see them, so I asked her to pose for a picture.

**MARTIN, SETH**
This is a photo of our first-born son, Ethan, at six weeks of age. We are new, excited parents who take a lot of pictures. We were very lucky to catch him at such an angelic moment.

**MASON, TONIE M.**
This is a photo of my then three-and-a-half-month-old, Carlene. We were out in our backyard garden one day admiring the flowers when I got the idea to put her in the flowerpot and capture the moment. I am a stay-at-home mom without any photography experience. I am capturing the lives of my daughters, Allison, twelve, and Carlene, now five months old, and my husband, Larry, who enjoys seeing new pictures of his daughters daily when he comes home from a hard day's work.

**MATHEW, SUBIN**
I come from a very laid-back cute little village in Kerala State ("God's our country" as they call it) in India. With this photograph, I intended to capture the serenity of my hometown with the brick and steel character of a city where I spent most of my life. The river, which represents the one flowing behind Perakathu, my house, and the sky, with an attitude, did well in enriching the picture's character. The bare branches of early spring underlined the effect. Birthday: May 1, 1971. Place: Kottarakkara, India. Parents: Thomas Mathew (Babu) and Leelamma Thomas. Brother: Jacob Thomas (Bibin). Education: T.K.M. College of Engineering; Quilon Computer Science and Engineering.

**MATTOS, FRANK**
This is a photo of my dog, Peaches. She loves to sit and watch the fish in our aquarium. Most of the time we put a chair in front of the tank so she can see them better. She will sit quietly for hours and follow the fish movements with her eyes, intently staring at them. I watched Peaches being born, and she was placed in my hand only minutes after her birth. Since that time, two years ago, she has become my best friend. She is a full-blooded Jack Russell terrier but doesn't behave like most Jacks, preferring to be with me and close to home.

She does not like to hunt even though we are surrounded by forest.

**McALPINE, BELINDA SUE**
The fog was deep, and we could not see a meter in front of our car. So ignoring the sign that said "Avalanche Area—No Stopping," we pulled over to take one last look at the snow and mountains prior to returning home to Australia. My photo was to be of a single tree and some ice-covered grass blades, but the heavens opened to provide us with this valley of mystery and beauty so far removed from our home in Australia.

**McBRIDE, MARY CATHERINE**
The beach provides a perfect background, giving one an opportunity to try skills as a photographer. This beautiful picture of my granddaughter, Alyssa, was taken on the beach in South Carolina. There is nothing more pleasurable than to view photographs of your grandchildren. The memories will last forever. I love you, Alyssa!

**McCOY, H. PENNY**
I feel that I see great photos through my eyes. I wish others to see what I see. This photo was taken at our annual Easter egg hunt. My personal quote for life is "stay happy, stay healthy."

**McDONALD, JON LEONARD**
I love to take pictures and then put the rolls of film in a ziplock in the refrigerator. When it gets full, I pull some out and take them for processing. I love the whole potluck of not knowing which pictures I will get back. They are always wonderful surprises you forgot you even took.

**McDONIE, JAMES D.**
I retired in 1999 from the Ohio Department of Transportation, and my wife went back to work part-time. She got me a new digital camera for Christmas that year so that I could take pictures to e-mail, put in letters and cards, etc. I've been taking pictures of family, friends, vacations, special occasions, and wildlife. Earlier this year my father-in-law gave me a squirrel-feeder to put in my backyard. As soon as I put the feeder up, they came to eat the ears of corn. I have squirrels, chipmunks, birds, and even an occasional rabbit or opossum.

**McFARLAIN, NATHAR RAY**
This "Cajun Cabin" photo was taken with a Nikon N-70 camera. The wood derrick next to the cabin is a replica of the first oil well drilled in the state of Louisiana. The photo was taken from across the small lake.

**McGINNIS, CLARENCE RAYMOND**
This photo is one of many my wife, Loeva, and I took of the wildflowers south of San Antonio, TX, this spring 2001. The Kodak used was a retirement gift from my co-workers at Southwest Research Institute. I enjoy photography—especially digital—working at church, and helping neighbors. My first attempt to reconstruct an old photograph (wife's grandparents) on my PC turned out great, and I'm currently working on another.

**McMAHON, HERBERT REPPARD**
This photo was taken in December of 1999 in the Tug Hill Plateau area of upstate New York. I used a Canon Elan II, Kodak E100VS slide film and a Tamron 70-210 2.8 lens with no filters of any kind. The camera was set aperture priority (2.8). I am always looking for the light, morning and evening, and a picture.

**MEDINA, FREDERICK ALBERT**
As this seagull gazed over the waters of Plymouth Harbor, one could sense that he was surveying his little slice of Heaven and contemplating his place in it. The young bird felt peace and contentment; he had it exactly right. Everyone should visit Plymouth, MA, with Ruthanne and our two cats. My parents, brothers, sister, and in-laws live nearby. I am employed by the Foxboro Company as an electronic test technician. I am blessed with five nieces and two nephews.

**MERCURI, DENISE MARIANNE**
One weekend I was sick, and my daughter, Jade (R), pleaded and begged for hours to watch my granddaughter, Alora. She finally said, "Listen, Mommy, I promise I'll do all the baby-sittin'. It's not a hard job." So . . . I laughed and gave in. Jade fed Alora, changed her diapers, entertained her, went for a walk, crawled all around the house with her, then repeated it all over again! Only a few hours had passed. By the time Alora's naptime came, Jade was so pooped out she fell asleep on the floor, too! It was the most perfect moment to capture.

**MESERVE, ROBERT H.**
Living in the granite state of New Hampshire gives me the opportunity to capture many beautiful seasonal photographs of its landscape. This picture, "New England Birches," was taken on the White Mountain Highway between Conway and North Conway, NH. I primarily take landscape photographs because of the beauty. This is a hobby I started five years ago, and I plan on continuing my quest for picture-perfect moments.

**MIHALCIK, MARIAN A.**
I have a desktop publishing business and work with a lot of pictures and graphics. This is my special intelligent cat named Tojo. He will look at a challenge and study it until he knows of how he's going to do it—and mostly gets it accomplished. If one of the other cats is eating, he will pull the bowl from under them and over to himself and eat the food. He's a leader and insists on getting his own way. His eyes are exceptionally large and when he's mad at me, the black centers are almost his whole eyes. He gets jealous when I give my attention to another cat; he pouts.

**MIHALCIK, MARIAN A.**
This is a photo of my Russian blue cat. She needed a home, so we took her in. She brought us a family of four kittens exactly like her, all the same color. We didn't want to part with them so we kept them all. I had my camera in my hand when I saw her sitting on a wall, so I snapped her picture, and it looks as though she posed for it. I have had offers for them but we won't part with

them. Precious found a good home for herself and her family.

**MIKHAIL, GEORGE R.**
I was born in Giza, Egypt, and moved to the United States of America fifteen years ago. Photography is one of my many hobbies. Recently, I started to scuba dive and was amazed with the beauty of the underwater world. So I thought you might enjoy this picture.

**MILLER, KEN S.**
I have taken many photos of hang gliders, but none have ever turned out as unique as "Silent Flight." This is a perfect example of being in the right place, in the right conditions, at the right time. I love the outdoors, wildlife, and extreme sports. My camera goes everywhere I go in hopes of capturing some of the unique moments I have seen or experienced. "Silent Flight" was taken in Lakeview, OR, during the United States Hang Gliding Association Nationals. I was perched under the launch pad as the gliders took off, with the sun directly overhead. I shaded the lens with my hand and took a series of shots. This is the only one that turned out.

**MILLER, LARRY**
I am an airline pilot and also a retired military pilot. As a result, I get "paid" to travel to many exotic places around the world. There have been many photographic opportunities during my travels. I really enjoy the possible different sunsets; however, in Rio a sunrise was the "possible" shot. This photo of Ipanema Beach was the result.

**MILLER, MISSY J.**
I love taking pictures of my children, and this one of my daughter, Avery, is a favorite. She was sixteen months old at the time, and it was her first Easter egg hunt. I love that I almost captured her thoughts when she grabbed these eggs and ran. She took off with them as if it was a race and then realized, "What do I do with these things anyway?" It was such a beautiful, yet realistic, picture of a child exploring the world around her.

**MILLER, SHERLYNN A.**
"Mighty Niagara" is truly one of the greatest wonders of the world. We snapped this picture during a family vacation to Niagara Falls just minutes from boarding the boat seen so small in the picture. Our whole family loves taking pictures. We can't wait to go on our next vacation! I am so proud and excited to be able to share them with you!

**MILTENBERGER, DEANA**
This is a picture of my husband, Tony, with our youngest daughter, Vanessa. I just love the way she laid her head against his chest, so trusting that he will always be there for her.

**MISHLER, JUANITA MARIE**
This photo was taken at my brother, Jeff's, home. We constructed a haunted house on his front lawn. We made a tripod out of large wooden poles, hung chains on it to hold a very large caldron, and filled it with water. We heated it from underneath and added dry ice to create a fog effect. The woman in front is my sister-in-law, Marilyn Peiffer, a true

wizard. The faint witch in the background is me, Juanita Mishler. The picture was taken using a timer. I love to take pictures and like to capture the most unique moments I can.

**MOHAMAD AL USTAD, SALEH AHMAD**
It used to be very easy to recognize whether a girl was married or not by whether or not she was wearing a veil. But to know if she is divorced is more difficult. I created a double image with a woman wearing the veil both on and off.

**MONTGOMERY, SHERRILL**
Bear and Lucy are German shorthair pointers. They are the grandchildren I'll never have. We live in the country, and they have a huge yard and their own pool. They are very interested in everything and everyone. I love taking pictures of them, as they are always into something. They think they are lap dogs. During the past year, we've lost their mother, Gretchen, and their uncle, Cash, a Dobie. Sometimes they get tired of me taking pictures and will leave the room or yard. I love taking pictures with my digital camera because I can "see" the picture now.

**MOORE, ELIZABETH ANNE**
I've been an avid photographer since the birth of my son thirteen years ago, when my sister gave me a nice 35mm camera for Christmas. My best friend, Kathy, taught me how to take a picture, capture a moment, and really pay attention to what I was photographing. I am also fortunate to be working for a digital photography-related company. I love what digital can do for the amateur. I had focused on the tree leaning and had forgotten about the horizon. I was able to straighten that out and get a really nice picture.

**MOORE, GERALD LEROY**
I live in Arizona with my wife, Jean, my adopted daughter, Rachell, and Ashley, a large white Lowchen. Although Nicky is no longer with us, he filled our lives with amazing love. Jean taught him to say mama. He lived almost eighteen years. This photo was taken after his bath, and he wanted to run. We called him "son." The little lion, Nicky, was one magnificent little guy. I am an aerospace planning engineer. Nicky was our son, and we miss him. The Lowchen is a very intelligent and lively breed.

**MOORE, RAYANNE**
This is a photo of my niece, Clare, born January 23, 2001, holding a photo of her daddy, Brad, born Sept 6, 1961. Not only is she the apple of his eye, but as you can see, she looks just like him! The parents are Brad and Vicki McGregor from Paducah, KY.

**MORGAN, EBERLE JANE**
This photograph reminds me of what is most important in my life: to express myself freely and joyously, feel the warm rays of love on my body, to let my creativity run with no deadline or agenda, and to be like a child on the beach, filled with wonder and awe at the beauty that is everywhere in everything in this universe. The children are my sons. The beach is Rhossilli Bay in Wales, where I've taken many memorable photographs.

**MORISSETTE, KARLYN RITA**
After my freshman year at Boston University, Rachel, Kristin, and I went on a road trip to visit Tyler in Erie, PA. All of us had lived on the same floor that year. Over the next week, I took over 125 pictures. This one was taken on our second day there, when we decided to watch the sunset on Lake Erie.

**MOYER, THOMAS**
On a Christmas visit to the grandparents in the snowbelt of Ohio, my daughter, Emily, had the chance to meet her e-mail pal from England. Zoe had never gone downhill sledding. Emily and her brothers, Sam and Jon, gave Zoe the front row seat on this first trip down the hill. I was pleased with the way the camera froze this moment in time. Their expressions range from excitement to fear to "I'm outta here if we start heading for the pond!"

**MULLINS, DELAINE DUNAWAY**
This precious photograph is of my two-and-a-half-month-old infant daughter, Bryanna DeLayne Mullins. Exhausted from a busy weekend with our family, her daddy and I were unable to awaken our baby girl for an Easter portrait. Expecting to disturb her slumber, I placed Bryanna in her Easter basket among the wildflowers in our backyard. She cuddled herself into this sweet position, allowing me to capture this precious moment.

**NAGY, A. T.**
I was raised in the foothills of the Austrian Alps, and as such I did a lot of hiking. Nature is at her finest here, and her beauty is unrivaled. Nature's creatures are determined and patient, and this spider's home sparkled radiantly in the early morning dew.

**NAVARRE, KEVIN RAY**
Who's afraid of the big bad wolf? With Smokey by my side, I'm not afraid of anything. Wolves have been given a terrible reputation because of ignorance. In our own way, we have tried to change the false ideas people harbor. Truth will prevail.

**NEVIN, ALEX**
Three months ago I quit my corporate job to pursue more creative endeavors. That I have been honored by being included in this anthology is extremely encouraging and gratifying. Thank you, Picture.com, for this wonderful opportunity. This picture is of my favorite pair of red sneakers. As you can see, I wore them to their grave. I took this picture at Balmoral Beach in Sydney, Australia, to remember them by. I would like to thank my parents for buying me my first good camera, and my sisters for their constant support and encouragement.

**NIEKOWAL, JAMIE AARON**
I like to take timed exposure photos like this one. Many times, I don't always get the results I want, but sometimes I get something like "Cast No Shadow." This shot was a spur-of-the-moment photo opportunity. My friend stopped and said, "I'll stand still." So I hit the cable release and held on for five seconds and then went back to class. The negative was flawless. I dedicate this

picture to Ed Nowak, my photo teacher. He introduced me to the law of reciprocity and the wonderful world of black-and-white photography.

**NOLTE, ROBIN M.**
I don't always see good shots when my camera is available, but this past winter when I visited my fiance, David, in northern New Jersey, accompanied by my German shorthair pointer, Gretchen, I couldn't pass this pose up. Gretchen thinks she is human as well as being an obvious member of the family, and this photo of her shows her personality plus! I came to own her by adoption from the local animal shelter where I resided before relocating to New Jersey. More people need to visit shelters for that perfect pet.

**NORMAN, ERICA RENEE**
This is a picture of my friend, Kati. I took this picture in my photography class after Kati had been having a very bad day. I think this photo really expresses how a lot of teens feel on any given day.

**NOWELL, ELAINE**
On a visit to my sister-in-law's in south Georgia, I was photographing roses in her botanical yard, fulfilling my hobby as an amateur photographer. As I turned, I noticed her beloved pets, a beagle named Trampas and a Labrador named Lady, sitting side by side watching me like spectators. Such a spectacle as it was, I laughed then shot this photo. They remained undaunted for some time just watching me.

**O'LANEY, DAVID MARK**
This photo was taken in the spring of 2000 while traveling through the Czech Republic. The castle is built on the steep banks of the Vltava River and towers over the narrow, cobbled streets of Cesky Krumlov. The historical town is remarkable with a fantastic photo opportunity around every corner! I chose this photo because I feel it best demonstrates the castle's dominating presence over the small Bohemian town.

**OAKES, JEFFREY L.**
This is a photo of a friend's son watching a Lionel train go by. What caught my eye was the smile on his face and his reflection in the window. I am a student photographer through NYIP.com and am hoping to make a career in photography. I am now thirty-nine and have been taking photos most of my life, mostly of nature here in Tennessee.

**OBERHOLTZER, JEANETTE**
This photo was taken at Phipps conservatory in Pittsburgh, PA, while the "Big Bugs" by David Rogers were on display. Snapping photos is a hobby of mine. I am a wife, mother of three great kids, and grandmother to six. I think God's creation is wonderful, and I thank him every day for the chance to enjoy it.

**ODOR, MARVIN R.**
This is an amazing portrait by the ocean that captures the essence of a divi-divi tree, the presence of death, and the vigor of life. The divi-divi tree in the portrait, which lived in the past, and the ocean, which is still living in the present, blend together to capture the elements of a majestic por-

trait. It also reflects the tranquility by the ocean. This portrait was taken in Aruba on the north coast of the island. This divi-divi tree is only found in the Caribbean.

**OLIVER, STELLA BERNADETTE**
This is a photo of my cat, Sylvester. He bears a striking resemblance to the Warner Bros. Sylvester. He was just sitting there, and I propped the soft toy next to him. He was unconcerned. The soft toy was a real primadonna; it kept falling over just as I was ready to take the shot.

**ONDRAJKA, ROSE K.**
Pistol was a Christmas present from my daughter. She is two years old and is very special to us. Her registered name is Pistol Packing Mama, and sometimes she lives up to her name. Pistol is one of the family and goes everywhere with us.

**ORSINI, GABRIELE**
Color, shadow, atmospheres, sensations—watching the world from the point of view of the light enhances the perception of reality. But photography operates a massive manipulation: it cuts a frame of the world, deleting anything out of that frame. Perspective and colors transform an experienced and abandoned thing into something completely different. Sometimes the same nature modifies itself according to a current imagery.

**PALMA, LINA**
Like one of many places we want to remember, Lake Tahoe was photographed for the love and beauty of nature. My family and I are very pleased with its original outcome and are much more proud that this was opportune for publication to share with you. This is dedicated to Daniel and Grace for letting us tag along on the trip to Lake Tahoe of March 2001.

**PANDOLFINI, ANTONIO BRUNO**
This is Stormy, an affectionate cat who was brought in during a thunderstorm. The photo was taken the day after Christmas 2000. He managed to lift the lid with his nose and climb inside. I caught him in the corner of my eye and went for my camera. As he peeked out, I snapped three photos. Not soon after the third picture was taken he jumped out.

**PANTHAKI, YAZDIE NOSHIR**
These two village kids at Vrindavan (the birth place of Lord Krishna) were fascinated by my Canon digital camera, and how they could see themselves in its display. I thought they looked so pure and innocent. The friend on the right was carrying a glass of milk back for his sister at home and said he would return shortly for more photographs to be taken of him and his friend. He said that if he did not finish his errand on time, his mother would scold him. The picture was overexposed by one stop. I processed my first roll of black-and-white film when I was thirteen years old, learning from a book that was in a makeshift darkroom, a neighbor's bathroom! I like candid portraiture and stage photography without the use of flash. Though I have been a flight attendant for the past twenty-two years, photography is and always will be my passion.

**PARKER, LINDA J.**
In 1993, a half mile off the coast of Key West, FL, on a tri-level glass-bottom boat trip, people on the third level threw cheese doodles into the water. I, on the second level, leaned over the side to shoot this feeding frenzy of yellow-tailed snapper.

**PASNIK, M. NANCY**
I am currently a stay-at-home mom of two children, ages three and one. I was eight months pregnant and cooking dinner one night when my daughter came running in exclaiming about two rainbows outside. I quickly took everything off the stove and waddled outside with my camera. This was the result.

**PAVLISH, KATHRYN ANN**
I took this picture of one of my best friends when we were on a high school band trip to compete in Orlando, FL. I like to shoot black-and-white photos to give realism to my shots. I thought she looked so reflective, so that's what I titled the photo, "Reflections On A Bus." I love shooting pictures, using different angles and cameras. I hope to become a professional photographer later, either in news reporting or for a magazine. Photographs are a great way to bring people together.

**PEREZ, HUGO**
This is a photo of Brenda and Johnathan. It is Brenda's quince años (fifteenth birthday), and Johnathan is her chambelan. I followed them around looking for the right opportunity. My goal was to catch a natural moment. I take my camera almost everywhere I go, from family get-togethers to the supermarket. I don't feel complete without it. I like to take pictures of people and of the city. I feel that I am documenting history. Photo opportunities are everywhere, and I don't want to miss one.

**PHILLIPS, ROBIN**
This picture was taken in the beautiful north Georgia mountains near my home where I grew up. This was one of my favorite spots to visit as a little girl, so I was delighted to catch this shot when I had taken my own daughters, Kristin, six, and Alli, two, to visit the area.

**PHILLIS, SARAH JANE**
I took this photo in the Hunter Valley near my old home. It was a beautiful spring day when I caught this horse on camera, emerging from the shadows of the creek bed, ghostly white in appearance. For me it is a very nostalgic memory, as it reminds me of walks up into the hills I would take with my family. I am currently studying visual arts in Brisbane. I love the feeling a photograph can inspire!

**PIERCE, RHONDA LOU**
This photo was taken as we were driving over the Intercoastal Canal in Gulf Shore, AL. My mother-in-law, Rose, was here for a visit, and Mother Nature was really showing her stuff. I was fumbling for my camera because I'm obsessed with sunsets, and Mama Rose handed me her camcorder. I was shooting video and still shots at the same time. I was lucky enough to get this perfect shot; although, as beautiful as this sunset was, it

wasn't hard to get a gorgeous picture. Thank you for allowing me to share this with others. Mother Nature is an awesome sight to behold!

## PIERPOINT, ANDREW MICHAEL
I took this picture from the airplane I was in while flying home for Thanksgiving. I got bored during the flight so I decided to play with my new camera. After a while, I looked out the window and saw the sun setting. I thought it would make a good picture . . . and there it is.

## PIETROBONO, HEATHER NICOLE
Jade is a registered Arabian mare who was kept mostly in a stall for about eight years with minimal human contact and training. My grandparents bought her in August 1999. While visiting my grandparents, I helped them feed the horses. I noticed Jade had finished eating and was peeking out her stall door. I took this picture because she just seemed so curious about her surroundings. Jade now has lots of tender loving care, green pastures, and is currently being trained for endurance riding.

## PIKUS, MICHAL
This is a photo from my business trip to the United States of America this year. I am a specialist in nature photography and have found paradise in many countries, including the United States of America (gold triangle), Scotland, Slovakia, and Iceland.

## PIZARRO, ADOLFO ESTEBAN
"Shh, it's a secret," says Fifi, the one-year-old kitten, to Genesis, also a one-year-old baby girl. Her proud parents are Alice and Joel Justiniano Orta. This picture was taken at a family reunion. I was taking pictures of Fifi when I noticed she had just jumped on top of the sofa where Genesis was resting. Instantly, as if by some kind of animal instinct, I knew that all I had to do was wait for the ideal moment to take the picture . . . and here it is. I hope you like it as much as we did. The whisper? Say cheese!

## PLAKANS, SHELLEY S.
Barbados has some of the most picturesque sunsets in the world. We were lucky to have a beautiful ship passing just as the sun was going down. We never get tired of these beautiful acts of nature.

## POWELL, MADONNA COMBS
This is a picture of my granddaughter, Jessica. She is always posing and definitely loves the camera. She will be ten years old on July 24th. My husband and I live in Johnston, SC, and have another grandchild, a little girl, who will be three in November. Her name is Karson. Jessica spends a lot of time with me, and I am always taking her picture. Maybe one day she will be a model. Jessica is in the fifth grade, plays piano, and, as you can see, she loves the great outdoors.

## PRIEST, MARGARET ANN
I'm a single mom with two girls. This is a picture of my new daughter, Mary. We almost lost her during birth, but she was strong and made it through. I love her very much. She's always doing funny things, and I had to run to get my

camera just to get this picture. Now I keep it near me all the time so I'll never miss a shot. I just finished college in April with an associates degree in computer information systems.

## QUIGLEY, BARBARA
At a recent family reunion camping trip at my brother, Allan's, cottage, I returned to my trailer to find these two visitors—my niece, Samantha Sullivan, and nephew, Matthew Heidman. They had stopped in to say hello and made themselves right at home! Best friends as well as cousins (children of of my sisters Pat and Caroline), they even had a mock wedding ceremony, thanks to officiators Kelsey and Stephanie Lusk.

## RATHBUN, CLAUDIA
My husband is a professional Santa Claus. His agency placed him in a mall just a three-hour drive from where my daughter lives, so she and her twin daughters, April and Autumn, came down for a weekend visit with us. While they were there, she and I took the girls to the mall to visit Santa. While we were waiting for his crew to get ready to take their picture, I took this picture with my Pentex IQ 200 zoom, 35mm camera. It came out better than either of the ones taken by the photo crew!

## RAYBION, BRENDA
This is a photo of my two-month-old granddaughter, Jayleigh. She was born in Texas and came to the Virgin Islands to visit me. This was one of the first baths I got to give her. I put in a little more bubbles than I meant to and this was the outcome. We call her Birdie because of the way she holds her mouth. All of the family told me this photo should be in a magazine. Well, she made it. She is such a good sport. Nana loves you, Birdie.

## REEVES, TERRY V.
This is a photo of Lachlan, my eldest grandson, hence the title "Grandma's First Love." I have been a keen photographer since I became a grandparent. I now have nine grandchildren who keep me running. This was my first attempt at black-and-white, and it was taken in Scrubland amongst the wiregrass on the side of a local reservoir. I was thrilled with the result; it is timeless and well reflects Lachlan's personality.

## REICH, FRIE M.
This is my grandson, Anthony, singing a song with his favorite character on Sesame Street, Elmo. He is our joy and constant new interest for my camera. It's digital and so much fun. It enables me to send pictures almost day to day to friends and family all over the globe. After my battle with cancer, I just enjoy life to the fullest. I love the flowers, I am mesmerized by sunsets, I try to see good in all people, and I forever keep my sense of humor each and everyday. Life is a present from God; all you have to do is take the box, open it, and look inside. You will be surprised.

## RESTIVO, CATHERINE
This photo was taken while I was on vacation in Egypt. A group of children were selling handmade dolls. I bought a few as gifts. This little boy had no dolls to sell, but offered his baby goat for

sale. As I couldn't bring a goat home, I took his photograph instead . . . for a nominal fee!

## REYNOLDS, WENDY
As time goes on, we tend to forget life's little moments. In order to remember these seemingly trivial occasions, I take pictures of everything, especially our kids, Jaimee Lee and Dalton. This is a photo of my daughter, Jaimee Lee, when she was just under six months old. Her daddy, Big Jamie, went out late one evening to purchase this super sauce. Whenever she was in it, she was in her own little world of color, sound, and taste. She especially loved to chew on the snail and therefore, in my eyes, this squeaky little toy was her version of escargot.

## RICE, DARLENE RUTH
This is what we woke up to every morning on vacation. It was the most spectacular view that anyone could ever have right outside their window. We go to Cape Hatteras, NC, every year for the best two weeks that anyone could want. It's so beautiful and peaceful just sitting on the beach fishing and watching the ocean. That's what nature is all about.

## RILES, ED
This photo was taken while on vacation in Colorado. I used an ordinary Minolta 35mm camera and slide film. Colorado is a beautiful state. At the time, I was working as an electronics technician for the FAA. I am now retired.

## RILEY, MICHELE RENEE
This is a photo of my niece, Rebecca. She's so full of life that this rare glimpse of peace seemed the perfect contrast. I cherish the joy she brings to my life. She's my "Peanut," and this picture warms my heart!

## ROBINSON, JENNIFER SHEILA
I have loved to take photographs since I was a young child, and, as a mother of four, I have especially enjoyed taking photographs of children. I like to get in close and capture the expressions on their faces. I was thrilled with this photo of my niece, Sarah. This was the first time we had met, and at first (as you can see in this photo) she was very shy with me, but curious I thought. She has beautiful red hair, cute little freckles dotted across her nose, and I feel she says a lot with her eyes.

## ROBINSON, MARK
This is a photo of me taken by me during a cold weather search-and-rescue operation. Why is it special? Normally a small group of searchers would be deployed in a small area. In this case one rescuer is deployed in the same area with a search grid and will search for twenty-four hours straight without stopping, staying in radio contact with command. I always take a camera on all the operations. I work as a martial arts instructor, survival guide, and I own an aerial photography business using radio-controlled helicopters.

## RODRIGUEZ, DANIELLE IRENE
This is my pet, Rat Stuart. Stuie is a very lovable and smart rat. He is very active. This is the only time I have ever been able to photograph him, for he will not sit still for a moment. Recently, Stuie

had a stroke and was completely paralyzed. She was treated for the stroke in a hyperbaric oxygen chamber and has almost completely recovered. Stuie is almost two years old. I have never entered any of my photos in a contest. I mostly like to draw and have won awards for my art/drawings.

### RODRIGUEZ, ELIZABETH
This photo is of my beautiful son, Javin. He is my only child and he means the world to me. When Javin was a baby, I would take pictures of him constantly, everywhere and anywhere. But in this particular photo, he got really scared of my stuffed gorilla. He would scream as loud as he could until I removed the teddy bear, but, regardless, I knew he was born to be in front of the camera. He is very photogenic. Once again, he's my everything. Thank you for the chance to see him in this publication. I'll treasure it forever.

### RODRIGUEZ, ORLANDO
This is a photo of Margie. She and I were on a cruise heading to Cancùn, Mexico, just enjoying the evening. We were in the elevator of the ship at the time and going up. I stood across from her and realized just how beautiful she looked as she stood there. I had to take the picture. Thanks to my camera, I now have the moment to treasure forever.

### ROEBUCK, LYNN
Caves are a unique and fragile environment. Many people do not venture underground, so they seldom ever experience the beauty. For those who will never see the wonders that are in caves, I have been capturing moments of unique beauty to share with others.

### ROEUN, PHIRUN
With an eye single to the glory of God. In this picture, it was my first time doing a lot of things. Since I'm from the East Coast, this was my first time stepping foot in the Midwest (in Nevada), my first time mountain climbing, first time on any mountain, and my first time gazing over a mountain to see the world as I've never seen it before. As you can see, that's me in the picture. It was a blessing to see God's creation from on high. Earth is beautiful!

### ROGERS, TIMOTHY ALEXANDER
Bradley, age five, loves to explore and discover new things. This picture was taken near our vacation house in Virginia on a nearby mountaintop trail. This was Bradley's first visit to the trail, and he could hardly contain his excitement. He strode far ahead of his parents, feeling nothing but joy and wonder in all of the new discoveries that nature had to offer. This picture captures the beauty, serenity, and innocence that Bradley experienced on that precious day. This was his first experience in being at one with nature. We are thankful to have captured it on film.

### ROOT, LORETTA
To whoever says that there's no God to be found, you're misled—he is all around (Phil Keaggy "Our Lives"). And sometimes he honors us by allowing us to trip the shutter and thus capture a reflection of his glory! I had never attempted time-lapse photography prior to this day and while shooting had prayed, "What good can come from leaving the shutter open so long?" Tears came to my eyes when I first saw the incredible beauty that was captured on my slides. How little of his total creation our eyes are capable of seeing. Baruch Atah Adonai, Eloheinu Meleca Ha' Olam!

### ROTH, JAMIN
Fritz, the inimitable "Weim," is caught here exploring the old corn crib on my father's pre-civil war farm home. Like a shadow enfleshed, Fritz is a constant companion when I visit my boyhood home in the Missouri Ozarks. The tones capture his intelligent, inquisitive, and vivacious nature.

### ROZZI, CAROL S.
It all started several years ago when we moved to a less populated area. Shortly thereafter, critters started coming into the yard. I asked my husband, Tony, "If we feed them, would more come?" He said sure! Well he was right. Our friends stopped over; they had their digital camera with them. There was a deer in the yard, and we were able to take pictures through the window. I was hooked. I then treated myself to a digital camera; that's how I captured "Backyard Wildlife." My sons, Thomas and Stephen, enjoy photographing as much as I do.

### RUBRIGHT, JENNIFER JOY
A wanderer by heart, often to the puzzlement of my friends and family, I find myself repeatedly jumping, usually headfirst, into things. Armed with a camera, the basic knowledge of my destination, and a wide-eyed, open-minded view of the world, off I go at the first itch to seek adventure. This was no different. I had heard about project G.R.E.E.N. (Global River Environmental Education Network) from a good friend of mine, and after persuasion on my part, found myself off to Guyana, a country that is simple, yet amazing beyond words. It was an experience that will live in my heart forever.

### RUSS, JAMES
I took this picture of my daughter, Grace, in the inner courtyard of First Presbyterian Church of Rogers, AR. My wife, our two children, and I had traveled almost a thousand miles to be with family to celebrate Easter Sunday. We listened to my sister-in-law preach the Easter sermon and stepped outside afterwards to enjoy God's handiwork. It was a beautiful sunny day with everything in bloom. I noticed my daughter playing with some petals and snapped off a camera shot. It has become one of my most cherished and inspirational pictures. Jesus has risen indeed!

### RUTHERFORD, LEAH ANDREA
In this picture, my daughter, Kyla, is just learning how to crawl and is very excited that she has it mastered, even if it is on her grandpa's bed. Parents need to take pictures soon and often for their kids. No matter what their kids may be doing, it's all memories.

### SALIN, DANIEL OTTO
For me, photography is like looking for gold: you never really know what you have until you see it in print, then there is a golden nugget before your eyes. I had to climb down snow-covered banks of the river to get under a bridge where I set up my tripod for the shoot. It was well worth the effort. I think I struck gold with this frozen fog day. Enjoy!

### SALVIA, VANESSA
This is an action photo of my daughter, Fiona. At the time, Fiona was two-and-a-half years old. A friend, Celia, had given her a box of candycanes for Christmas, and Fiona just couldn't get enough. This was an unplanned photo. I just happened to be ready at the right moment!

### SANTELLI, ANDY M.
Our cat, Austin, and his sister (not pictured) had a rough start in life. My husband and I went to Austin, TX, for a long business trip. On our first night at the hotel, we witnessed two beautiful baby kittens get tossed out of the window of a speeding car. The local shelters were full, and that's when we knew these two babies would now become part of our family. They flew as carry-on baggages on five different flights to come home with us to Nantucket Island! We all had quite an excursion. They're very popular flyers!

### SANTIAGO-CHRISTIAN, ELIAS
This is a photo of the monument to the Puerto Rican Jibaro at the rest area beside highway #52 in Cayey, Puerto Rico. It is one of my first digital photographs. I guess I was at the right place at the right time. It was truly a beautiful day. There was no reason for me to stop and shoot this picture that particular day. That is until I saw the photo!

### SCHOR, SUZI
My Tina has run my home for eight years, along with my maltese, Bogart. My horses are a different story! I live in an apartment. I'm a fan of photography, animals, and my daughter, Kate. I catch their wonderful attitudes.

### SEVEK, MARY RENEE
This is a photo of my great nephew, Indy, after his bath. I took the photo with my digital camera and was surprised the flash didn't go off. When I opened the photo up on my computer to look at it, I was glad the flash didn't work. The lighting was perfect and the photo was a once-in-a-lifetime shot.

### SEVIN, LAURIE L.
This is a picture of my oldest child, Lindsay, and my youngest, Shelby. I was in the back doing laundry. Her daddy asked her to hold her sister while he ran out the front door to check the mail. When I came in the living room, this is the moment I caught. She was waiting for him to come back quickly. When we got the picture back, Lindsay noticed the reflection. I explained to her that it was her and Shelby's guardian angels watching over them.

### SHAPIRO, GREGG
Winter on Maui is all about golf, beaches, relaxation, and whale-watching. While scanning the ocean surface for yet another blatant sign of these huge visitors, nature presented me with this gift.

**SHARPE, KRISTEN**
My three-and-a-half-year-old daughter, Jordan, wanted her picture taken with her brother, Stephen. She was trying so hard to hold him and keep him still. He thought it was more fun to laugh and try to squiggle away! They ended up laughing together and getting silly. I was lucky to capture this moment. My true passion is taking pictures of my children and creating scrapbooks with the photos.

**SHATTUCK, PAMELA D.**
This is a photo of my daughter, Hannah, experiencing chocolate pudding for the first time. The look on her face after making this mess was so priceless; it was like she was telling me how proud she was.

**SHEAR, KATHY**
I took this picture of my five-month-old son, Alexander Milton Shear. Alex always opened his eyes wide as an infant. I was so surprised to have captured the moment. Becoming Alex's mom has brought me more joy than I ever imagined it would, and I am always trying to photograph the most precious times.

**SHEARER, JOHN CLARE**
This is a photo of "Land's End," the very southern tip of the Baja Peninsula, taken while on vacation in Cabo San Lucas, Mexico. When we got home and looked at our photos, I realized that this one was almost identical in perspective and scale as a souvenir postcard we brought back with us. Comparing the two, I think that my photo is better, as it has richer colors and the details are more pronounced with the shadows and light. When not vacationing, I work as a paramedic in Abbotsford, about a forty-minute drive east of Vancouver, BC, Canada.

**SHEHEANE, ROBIN**
This is a photo of my beautiful sons, Shannon and Seth. They are dressed up for a Halloween outing. The excitement on their sweet little faces captures how we all felt when we were young. They are my world, and I pray that they keep the excitement for the rest of their lives.

**SHELTON, DEBBY**
I very much enjoy the great outdoors. This photo was taken at 6:45 A.M. out on Lake Sawyer in Black Diamond, WA. Mt. Rainer was magnificent on a very rare clear day.

**SHIELDS, MIKE W.**
It was December 19, 2000, and we were at the hospital for a check-up. My wife was pregnant and due any day with our second child. We were sadly ushered out with a notion that the time was soon, but not now. While leaving the hospital, we noticed the most incredible cloud pattern. We were thrilled to grab this photo. With my back on the ground, I tried to get as much of the sky as possible. These clouds stretched across the entire sky! We viewed this as sort of our personal kick-off to the day's events. Our ten-pound baby boy was delivered later that afternoon. Kevin, this is for you!

**SHOU, EVA**
Lily, sweet, sweet girl . . . given up by her owners only because she had developed separation anxiety. She is also one of a few that I had the opportunity to care for as a foster parent for a pet adoption agency. Working to help rescued dogs find homes has become very rewarding; seeing life reappear in their eyes, their smile, and their trust is more than anyone can hope for.

**SILVA CANALE, PAOLA J.**
This picture makes me remember my trip to Marco Island, FL, while I was spending some days there for vacation. The sunsets are great and I always love to take pictures of the sea and all of nature. So I think this is a good shot. I wish I could take better photographs each time and maybe sell them; this would be a dream come true.

**SINGH, DALJINDER**
The wildflowers at Big Bend in March 2001 were the best they've been in the last ten years. This photo was taken without any filters with a Nikon 80-200mm AF f12.8 lens with a close-up ring attachment, Nikon F100 camera and tripod. It was late afternoon, and the spines kept on getting in the way of the composition. It worked out in the end. I am a software professional, and photography is one of my serious hobbies.

**SIZEMORE, GINGER**
Out of the corner of my eye, I saw a little green thing whipping around in a panic. I took a closer look; it seemed to be just a tail showing from the plant. A little creature was caught head down in a very tight plant and was trying to get out. I carefully lifted it up and saw it was a very colorful day gecko. The colors were so incredible I just had to take a picture. I'm always looking for inspiration to use in my art, which includes photography, computer art, beading, and teaching online needleweaving classes. Mom would have enjoyed seeing this little critter.

**SMITH, GLORIA DOROTHY**
I like taking pictures and am often teased about the angles I put my body into to get certain shots. I believe this photo was one such time. The haying was done for this sweltering summer day in 1982 in the small farming community of Gordondale, AB, where my mother and father-in-law lived. My husband, Doug, his brother, Marty, his wife, Brenda, and I drove all the kids to the dugout to cool off. Our daughter, Krista, and her cousin, Josey, were a little bit ahead of us when I saw the picture and asked Krista to take Joe's hand.

**SMITH, MARK STEVEN**
I was at a town function when it began to rain, and being on a boat, I thought I should get home. By the time I got to the middle of the lake, I was looking at the sunset you now see. I was very lucky to be at the right place at the right time.

**SNIDER, VICKY L.**
This picture was taken from my living room window. It is of our first snowfall in 2000. We received nine inches of snow. As I stood looking out, I thought of what a pretty picture it would make. So I grabbed my camera and took a few pictures. I liked this one the best and am thrilled to have it published.

**SO, STEFENES**
This is a photo of my lovely daughter, Kayleen, having a restful evening at the Kota Legenda Estate, Cibubur. When I have a digital camera, I take photos often, especially to capture the moments in life as well as special occasions because they will live forever. We love looking at and sharing photos with family and friends.

**SONCK, GEERT**
About ten years ago, when I visited the U.S. for the first time, I was deeply impressed by the many strange rock formations I saw; they all seemed to hide their own true stories just for themselves. Year after year, I went back there and every time one wonder of nature surpassed the other in its beauty. "The Bridge" seemed to be a link between the new world and nature itself. From the many pictures I have taken, I've chosen this one as the most exact copy of nature towards progress.

**SORRELL, DANA D.**
This photo was taken near Wilmington, NC, while my husband and I were on vacation. We thought it was humorous, as there were other gulls hovering around those perched on the pilings.

**SOUDER, CHARLOTTE ELAINE**
My husband and I drove the truck and were on our way to Las Vegas for a delivery. This photo was taken on March 4, 2001, at around twelve noon. I have taken photos across the United States, but the "Hoover Dam" was breathtaking. Just imagine what it took to construct this landmark.

**SPAULDING, JON K.**
I used to hunt animals, and now I no longer hunt with a rifle. I believe that all living things have a soul. I even threw the bass in the photo back into the river because I didn't want to kill it. As I've grown older, I've realized life is a precious commodity. I now do my hunting with a camera. I was born in Lake Charles, Los Angeles. My father was in the air force. I am the third child of six children. I have lived in many places, but Vermont is my home. I had my mother write this for me because I have severe dyslexia and sometimes need her help.

**SPENCER, DAREN HARLOW**
This is a photo of the historic "Geiser Grand" Hotel in Baher City, OR, which has been completely restored. I have been a photographer for fourteen years. My most recent endeavors include designing web pages, graphic design, creating art from my images, and creating custom private labels for bottled water. My photography reflects my belief that to the attentive eye, every moment of each season, Mother Nature's artistry beholds, every hour, a picture that was never seen before and will never be seen again.

**SPRADLIN, VIRGINIA CARMEL**
I was born in West Germany and have lived in many places; but I must say I think Virginia has the most beautiful scenery of all. I would say this even if it wasn't my home. I decided years ago to

find something to do that I enjoyed; this led me to take photography classes where not only did I find a great hobby, but I also met the man of my dreams, Dean. After the class was over, we got married. The rest is a beautiful portrait. He is all the inspiration I need.

**STAMBAUGH, MARY**

This picture was taken at my parents' house on Christmas Day. I was walking around snapping pictures when I spotted my mother and daughter on the floor, oblivious to everything around them. When the two of them play together, it's always as if they're alone, even in a crowded, noisy room. Everyone deserves a friend like that.

**STEELE, PAM JEAN**

Every year in May, my feathered friends show up out of the blue and build a new home to raise their young. Last year the parents brought their adult children, and I had two wonderful nests to watch come to life! The parent birds built their home on my flood light, while the young couple started their family in the bunkhouse for supplies. I feel lucky to share their world.

**STEIES, T. J.**

This picture was taken through the window of my home in east central Iowa. I live on a hill overlooking the Iowa River Valley. Although some dislike winter, I find that it has a beauty. This picture shows just one of the wonderful things to see in an "Iowa Winter."

**STEWART, SHARON K.**

The little girl is my granddaughter, Kalie Le Force. She was visiting for the weekend, rocking her baby and singing "Rock-A-Bye Baby." I took this picture not for any special reason. Like all the other pictures I take of her, I don't want to lose one precious moment or any little thing she does. Just to be a part of her life is worth all the riches in this world to me; and she is beautiful, isn't she?

**STICK, THERESE**

My free-spirited girl is always happy and singing. Her eyes open and a smile beams always. This was a random shot to capture her nature with a 35mm Pentax 1Q zoom 700. Ashley is truly a free-spirited, happy child, age eight, and this photo reflects her personality.

**STRAATMANN, JASON ERIC**

This photo represents several major features of Warrensburg, MO: the B2 Stealth Bomber flying overhead from nearby Whiteman Air Force Base, the historic Johnson County Courthouse, and ill-fated Old Drum. Old Drum, a prized hunting dog, is the original Man's Best Friend, a title given to him in court as his owner's attorney (Senator George Graham Vest) battled with a neighbor over Old Drum's untimely death by gunfire when he crossed the neighbor's property in 1870. Last, but certainly not least, Rie, after I complete my PhD and you finish your degree, would you marry me? I love you!

**SUDENTAS, ALFONSO**

Animals can take on human-like expressions. This is Buster after committing high crimes and misdemeanors; he has been properly reprimanded.

**SUGGS, KATHY L.**

I never leave home without it—my camera, that is! I took this picture of our son, Tyson, pictured here at five months, and the cat on our way to Grandma and Grandpa's house during the Christmas 2000 holiday season. Daddy drove and I sat in the back with Tyson and played peek-a-boo. Whenever I look at this photo, I feel like I'm right next to him in the car. His eyes are filled with dependent love, so trusting, so innocent, so happy.

**SULTON, JENNIFER**

This is a photo of my nephew, Ryan, my great-niece, Britinee, and nephew, Brenton. I was baby-sitting them when this picture was taken. They were trying to behave so that I would take them to Walmart for a toy. The key word for them was "trying." I love taking pictures and keep my camera loaded and ready. I like taking pictures of the unexpected as well as the expected. I've never taken pictures as a profession, though I would like to do it professionally. I've been taking pictures for a long time.

**TAI, KOHEI**

My grandfather was a photographer, and he gave me a camera when I was in a secondary school. That's the beginning of my photographic experience. This is a photo of the "Sydney Opera House," which symbolizes Sydney. It shines like jewelry in the dark black sky, with which many people are fascinated. I am from Japan but live in Sydney to study aviation. Thanks go to my father, mother, sister, and especially to my grandfather for supporting me.

**TAYLOR, ADRIENNE LISA**

My son, Zach, was about six months old in this picture. Its perspective made me reflect on all that he and I have been through together since the day he was born. I am greeted by his beautiful smile each morning, and I know that I am very blessed to have him in my life. I am a single mom and would not trade that for anything in the world because it has strengthened my spirit and has made me proud of who I am. I plan to cherish every moment because all too soon today will be the reflection.

**THARPE, JAMES**

Actually, the Chihuahua and the cat are the best of friends. I built this three-foot tall stand in my front yard so that Mogi, the Chihuahua, could see over a short brick fence. The cat naturally went for the roof and the two of them normally look like a well-trained and alert team of spotters. On this occasion, Mogi was feeling sleepy, and her expression just seemed to be a plea to be left alone.

**THOMPSON, DEBORAH SIOUX**

Echo is my purebred Arabian horse. I have been fascinated by Arabians for as long as I can remember. Their intelligence and eagerness can be seen so clearly in the depths of their eyes. They each have their own unique personality that is truly amazing. When I gaze into Echo's eye, I remember this saying by R. B. Cunningham Graham: "God forbid that I should go to any Heaven in which there are no horses."

**THOMPSON, JENNIFER J.**

The word amateur definitely describes me. I have always enjoyed taking pictures but not as much as now. My son, Devin, is my inspiration. I love capturing his life on film and looking back on how far he has come. In this picture, Devin was around one year old. It was taken at a cabin in Minnesota; he appears to be fishing but is actually swinging a stick like a bat. He loves his baseball! I can only pray that I will someday inspire him as he has me.

**THORNTON, JESSICA A.**

I am twenty-two years old and come from a rather large family. Mom, Dad, six boys, two girls, one grandson, and one granddaughter make up this pack. One September afternoon some of us ventured out to look for pumpkins for Halloween. We found this neat little place in Lawrence, KS, that was overflowing with pumpkins. In this picture, my four-year-old son (the dark-haired boy) and my three-year-old brother, Sadj, (who is Alex's uncle!) show off their exhausted smiles!

**THOROLFSSON, HAUKUR**

Being a bird-lover from Iceland, finding myself two hundred miles south of the Falkland Islands with a Nikon FE with Micro Nikkor 55mm lens, I had awaited the chance to get exactly this picture for two months. There were sunsets but no Albatross, and plenty of Albatross on rainy days; finally I got it combined. Thank you for sharing this moment with me.

**TILIANDER, VERONICA SOFIA**

If I were to choose one picture to represent where my heart is placed in the camera, this one of my daughter, Sara, is artistically and lovably the one I like the most. All of my work as an amateur photographer shows that the subject of children, where there's a richness of spontaneous deep feelable moments, is where I perform the best.

**TINTNER-BISHOP, JANE**

My husband was sitting at the end of the couch reading the comics. When he got up to do something, he returned to find Cracker in his place reading the comics. Cracker's favorite comic is *Mutts*, and his least favorite is *Garfield*.

**TOWLER, GLENN RICHARD**

Celebrating the century of the Emu Bay Railway Company, this photo was taken at the top of the Rhyndaston tunnel in Tasmania's Coal River Valley on the final leg of a round Tasmania journey. "Clear Tunnel" shows the former Tasmanian government railway's Pacific Class (4-6-2) Steam Locomotive M4 as it comes out of the top of the tunnel. This photo captures the superb beauty of a steam-powered locomotive, showing steam and smoke as it struggles up this steep one in forty grade over the three quarter mile length of the tunnel. My photography captures many subjects, mainly of ships and trains.

**TRACY, PATRICIA GENE**

This photo was taken at the St. Louis Zoo. People are my favorite subjects. The child is my granddaughter, who was fascinated with the fallen leaves. Mom and Dad were helping her explore her world. My husband, daughter, and granddaughter are what make my world go round, and I can never have too many photos of them. Mom and Dad are both in the air force, serving short tours overseas. Belle lives with me, giving me plenty of opportunities to take photos. What an honor to have made it this far doing something I love.

**TRAN, LIZA TRANG**
This picture will live forever within me. This special moment was taken while I was hiking. It was so calm and peaceful. The Mountains, the trees, the river, the snow, and the clouds make a great combination don't they? Close your eyes and imagine you are there with a light breeze, and the sun shining down on you. Now that is where you want to be when you want time to yourself; no one can ever bother you at that moment. Every time I look at that picture, I feel that I am out there once again. And that I will always remember because I took that moment with me.

**TRANGGONO, MARGARET**
I woke up Christmas morning (2000) at my boyfriend, Gerald Foster's, house in Laconia, NH, and walked into the dark living room, dimly lit by the brightness of the snow. Florrie, the Kerrison family's cute and charming West Highland terrier was peacefully lying on the armchair, eyes closed. She heard my camera turn on and immediately arose to look at me. Coming from Singapore, that Christmas was my first traditional Christmas day with family mass, an ornament-covered tree, tons of presents, chocolate cake, roasted turkey, and lots of love. I will never forget it!

**TWYMAN, LINDA LORINE**
Two-year-old Katie was given a second chance at life. Katie was diagnosed with ASD, a birth defect involving the heart. She had open-heart surgery on December 19, 2000, at Doernbecher Children's Hospital in Portland, OR. Dr. Ungerleider was the miracle worker performing the flawless two-and-a-half-hour surgery. To assist Katie in coping with the psychological ramifications of such an invasive procedure, Doernbecher donated surgical items for her to play with. This was to ensure that Katie's mind and body healed to its maximum potential. It is true what they say; "Children are a gift!" I will always treasure mine!

**TYRRELL, EILEEN DAPHNE**
A friend and I last saw each other in Singapore forty-five years ago. Both of us now residing at the opposite ends of Canada met in London, England. Being somewhat overcast, we decided to visit the Imperial Luar Museum. Upon finishing our tour, we stepped outside to discover there had been a light shower. Walking along the path, I saw a display of the Peace Rose. Although I entitled the photograph "Peace Rose No. 2," I think with the upheaval in today's world I much prefer the name "Tears For Peace."

**UNSON, FRANCIS MICHAEL**
Like many UC-Santa Barbara and Santa Barbara City college students, I made my way towards the beach in time for the afternoon sunset. Clouds from the previous day's rains still lingered, resulting in the sun's glorious coronation. Incidentally,

the sunset photo is one of the first nature photos I have taken with a non-disposable camera. Given the remarkable results, I will most likely not return to my old picture-taking ways.

**VELASQUEZ, ROSIE**
Since the day Isabella was born, her older sister of just seventeen months, Magdalene, welcomed her into the family. Each day I watch them grow older and closer together. Although every moment isn't as calm as the one I captured here, they really understand what sisterhood is all about.

**VESTAL, LESLIE DENISE**
This is a photo of my two-year-old nephew, Tanner. He is such a very busy little fellow most of the time. It's hard to capture him on film, but when he stopped to smell a bouquet of artificial roses in my living room, we couldn't resist. I treasure this picture for many reasons, one being he's my precious nephew, the other being how difficult it is to catch him on film like this since he would much rather be playing in a puddle with tractors and trucks.

**VIEIRA, FÁBIO LUCIANO**
This is a photo of Cancún's sea. I saw this photo in my mind and just clicked; and here it is. I love the sea, and this moment will live forever.

**VIRZI, DAVID**
As a father of three beautiful daughters, my photo opportunities are endless. Even on a cold winter night, I was able to catch my daughter's enthusiasm as she built an igloo. I think the title "Exploring A New Home" helps to capture the vivid imagination of a ten-year-old. I love photography and hope to pass on my love for the art to my daughters.

**VITELA, ALFONSO**
It was an early afternoon this spring in a local Fort Worth park when I walked across one of its bridges. Suddenly I was struck by this lovely scene. A running creek, back lit, glistening water, surrounded by a variety of beautiful trees. I had to capture the moment. What accounted for its charming appeal? It's simple beauty that evoked in me a feeling of inner peace. So many of us are caught up with life's many pressures and busy pace. It's of little wonder that this picture is a success, for we all need moments of serenity.

**VOSS, EDD**
For the last twenty-eight years, my first love has been photography. This image was found while driving a semi-truck to support my photography. Now my work may support itself. It would be the achievement of a lifelong dream.

**WALL, KATHY ALMA**
Our North American history is slowly being eroded to make way for civilization. This photo was taken when such an occurrence was taking place. The uniqueness of the site was destroyed for a four-lane highway. This photograph represents the memory of what once was!

**WALLER, MARK H.**
This picture is a sign from the heavens and my Uncle Sidney. The Easter before he died, my

uncle and I were shopping, and I saw a vase of red tulips. I asked him to stop so I could purchase the flowers. He said we didn't have time then but would come back later. Later never came. He became ill not long after the shopping spree, but never forgot those red tulips. One of the last things he said to me was that he would get those red tulips one way or another. That was July, and he left us in August. The months passed, and spring arrived. I looked out my door one morning to find the yard was filled with red tulips! It was truly a sight to behold, and it brought me to tears. I know you're out there somewhere, Uncle Sidney, and I thank you from the bottom of my heart.

**WARD, SUZANNE**
This is my husband, Eric, holding our six-month-old daughter and first child, Madeline, who is my favorite subject to photograph. She is so lucky to have had the opportunity to bond so closely with her daddy in the first seven months of her life. Eric spent days caring for her. This was a totally spontaneous moment that I captured, and I am so glad that I did because it will always remind me of their special closeness. She will always be Daddy's little girl!

**WATT, NIK**
Photography is important. It breaks down barriers and brings people together, literally. Folk have visited here because of my landscapes. This is the wee doggie I bought my mum. He was in a rescue center. It saddens me that something so innocent and cute could be abandoned. Those who are cruel should suffer the same agony they administer. Alfie has added to our lives, and I love him to bits!

**WEINSTEIN, DEVYN MARIE**
This is my Siamese-Himalayan cat, Tylo. He really isn't getting sick, but actually is drinking out of the toilet! He and my bulldog, Booyaa, are best of friends. Tylo mimics everything Booyaa does, which is why he is drinking out of the toilet, because he watched Booyaa do it. Tylo will also only drink out of Booyaa's water bowl (I haven't filled Tylo's water bowl in over a year). From the day I brought Tylo home, I have always said that he is more of a dog than a cat, and now that he has a dog playmate, he feels more in touch with his true self. If any of you have ever seen the comic strip *Get Fuzzy*, that is an exact portrayal of Tylo, a psycho kitty. Although I am not a professional photographer, I think I did a pretty good job at capturing this moment.

**WEISSMAN, LISA**
Of all the subjects in the world to photograph, none are as beautiful or breathtaking as my children. Watching them experience the simplest wonders fills me with awe and inspires me to grab my camera to capture the moment so we can hold on to it forever.

**WELKER, KRISTY**
This photo, taken on the Logan River Trail near Logan, UT, is of our young German shorthair pointer. This photograph is unique in that it captures Rupert's free-spiritedness. The bloodhound-like characteristic that makes him a great hunter

can also create an interesting photograph. Many times we have witnessed this wild, macabre look—Rupert at top speed, running to catch up because he had stopped to follow game scent, or just hanging back in playful mischievousness so he could sprint past us. Whatever the motive may be, the look is always unmistakably "Rupert."

**WELLS, DONNA L.**
This photo was taken off the coast of Oregon while reuniting with long-lost siblings. This was my first visit there. I love to travel and take pictures of buildings, structures, landscapes, anything that depics/portrays the place I'm visiting. I'm addicted to photography and love sharing my favorite images with anyone who's interested.

**WELLS, LINDA SUE**
This is a photo of my grandson, Alec, at ten months old; he's one of three. Alec was enjoying his fudgesicle so much that I had to get my camera. Photography has been a lifelong hobby. I have always loved taking pictures of my children, and now I have so much fun taking photos of my grandsons. My daughter, Echelle, has blessed me with two grandsons, Tyler and Alec. My son, Brandon, has blessed me with my youngest grandson, Jaden. They bring me so much joy. I always have film in my camera. I never want to miss one of those special moments.

**WICAL, ANN MARIE**
This is our daughter, Eleanor Eileen Wical. This tiny angel is the joy of our lives, and this tender smile melts our hearts every day.

**WILLIAMS, MICHAEL WAYNE**
A friend who was acquainted with the great man gave me this book as a gift. To add a catalog feel to the picture, I draped my watch over the cover. The time and date on the watch face were accurate at the moment of exposure believe it or not!

**WILLIAMS, NORMAN**
Living in California, I have the unique opportunity to capture many awe-inspiring shots. With this shot, however, it was beauty and innocence in their simplest forms: man's best friend and a true princess sharing tender moments in time. Thus I chose to entitle this shot "Kiss From A Friend."

**WILSON, NELSON LEE**
Kayla and Caitlin celebrated their first birthday in January 2001. On that day, they came over to visit with Gran-Momma and Poppa. They were playing out of their resident box of toys when I caught them by surprise with this one.

**WINNIE, CHERYL FAWN**
This is a photograph of my daughter, Samantha. I am a seamstress, not a photographer. This is my favorite picture that I have taken of her.

**WISNIEWSKI, CHARLES**
It happens upon a common corner, seen by many a tourist or residential lover of the countryside, curving roadways that expose a new theatrical scene at any moment and . . . bang! He captures the quaint, sometimes jaded, image of something often taken for granted—a hometown everyday

occurrence that for the local folk and the Charlies of the world is appreciated. The all too familiar gray pavement takes on a new life as we pulse down the roadway to the next destination—hopefully with Charlie at the helm. To see such a common sight and find inspiration is unique. Thanks, Chaz!

**WOODLIEF, SHARON LEE**
I had just purchased a digital camera. It was on a night in the middle of winter during a storm when I walked outside to try and get a picture of lightning. All of a sudden I saw the moon, which looked like it had a face around it. When I put the disc in my computer and saw this photo, I thought it was really unique. I am married and have three grown children and four beautiful grandchildren. I own a five-acre ranch in Valley Springs, CA. I have five horses; two of them are miniature horses. I plan to raise and sell miniature horses.

**YATES, BRUCE GEOFFREY**
This is Brianne at the playground, upset that she couldn't play soccer with her cousins. My niece is so photogenic. I can't help but take photos of her every time I see her. Wide eyes and gracious poses come together every time for a perfect shot. She will make me famous!

**YOUNG, DONNA-MICHELLE**
A mind's eye takes millions of its own pictures and stores them to the delight of their master. This is my vision of serenity at near dusk "On The Bayou," so I decided to share it with the world. There are thousands of portrayals of the Bayou, but this one is certainly a pretty picture. If I make you smile, capture it in your memory and you will smile forever.

**YUZON, ERIC**
This was a very interesting architectural photo opportunity. The equipment used was a Canon Elan II with a 28-105 lens, which was mounted on a tripod. I used a long shutter speed of ten seconds. There was quite a breeze blowing. Notice the plants on the left side showing some motion. I bring my camera whenever I travel to other countries. Other photography includes candids of my family, studio portraits, stills, motor sports, creative weddings, and digital work. I hope to build a home studio in the future. Photography is my self-expression of the way I see people and the world.

**ZELLER, DIANA LEIGH**
This is a picture of my daughter, Loriell. It was taken at Halloween time on a trip to the pumpkin farm. When asked to choose one pumpkin, she simply replied, "I Want That One And That One And That One . . . ."

**ZIDE, PAMELA ANN**
My husband, Jeff, and I were celebrating our anniversary in Orlando, FL. While there we visited Sea World. I've always loved manatees and was so excited to actually see them up close! Naturally when the baby decided to nurse, I just had to take a picture. Who could resist?

**ZIMMER, LORI ANNE**
The American pit bull terrier suffers a bad reputation thanks to some irresponsible breeders and owners. If bred and socialized properly, a pit bull can be a loving, loyal, and playful family pet, as we've learned from our beloved Niquita. This photo from the summer of 2000 shows Niquita at eight weeks old, taking a dip in the Conodoguinet Creek. She didn't enjoy it much, whining pitifully the entire time. I think the expression of abject dismay on her face is simply priceless. It plainly says, "Yuck! Whose idea was this, anyway?"

# INDEX OF PHOTOGRAPHERS